HIKE
DEATH VALLEY

Hike. Contemplate what makes you happy and what makes you happier still. Follow a trail or blaze a new one. **Hike.** Think about what you can do to expand your life and someone else's. **Hike.** Slow down. Gear up. **Hike.** Connect with friends. Re-connect with nature.

Hike. Shed stress. Feel blessed. **Hike** to remember. **Hike** to forget. **Hike** for recovery. **Hike** for discovery. **Hike.** Enjoy the beauty of providence. **Hike.** Share the way, The Hiker's Way, on the long and winding trail we call life.

HIKE DEATH VALLEY

BY
JOHN MCKINNEY

TheTrailmaster.com

HIKE Death Valley By John McKinney

HIKE Death Valley ©2022 The Trailmaster, Inc. All rights reserved. Manufactured in the United States of America. No part of this book may be used or reproduced in any manner whatsoever without written permission except in the case of brief quotations embodied in articles and reviews.

Acknowledgements: Thanks to the many rangers and park staffers who've reviewed my writings over the years with a special shout-out to Charlie Callagan, Wilderness Coordinator, Death Valley National Park.

ISBN: 978-0934161-90-9
Book Design by Lisa DeSpain
Cartography by Brandi Webber
HIKE Series Editor: Cheri Rae

Published by Olympus Press and The Trailmaster, Inc. TheTrailmaster.com (Visit our site for a complete listing of all Trailmaster publications, products, and services.)

Although The Trailmaster, Inc. and the author have made every attempt to ensure that information in this book is accurate, they are not responsible for any loss, damage, injury, or inconvenience that may occur to you while using this information. You are responsible for your own safety; the fact that an activity or trail is described in this book does not mean it will be safe for you. Trail conditions can change from day to day; always check local conditions and know your limitations.

Contents

Introduction 9

Death Valley National Park 14

Eureka Valley, Scotty's Castle & Racetrack Valley

Eureka Dunes 23
  California's highest dunes, impressive for their size and silence

Scotty's Castle 27
  Tour an amazing desert hacienda, walk the Windy Point Trail

Ubehebe Crater 31
  Hike the cinder-covered rim of a volcanic crater

Ubehebe Peak 35
  Grand vistas from the crest of Last Chance Range

Racetrack Valley 39
  Walk around the weird: rocks that race around when we're not looking

Stovepipe Wells and Beyond

Titus Canyon 45
  Twisting narrows of high-walled canyon

Fall Canyon 49
    Less visited neighbor to Titus Canyon

Death Valley Buttes 53
    From Hells Gate to grand views of the central part of the park

Mesquite Flat Dunes 57
    Fun in the sun on easy-to-reach sand dunes

Mosaic Canyon 61
    Mosaics of colorful rock fragments adorn marble walls

Salt Creek 65
    Boardwalk nature explores habitat of the Salt Creek pupfish

Furnace Creek & Amargosa Range

Golden Canyon 71
    Interpretive Trail illustrates Death Valley at its colorful best

Zabriskie Point and Gower Gulch 75
    Past Red Cathedral and golden Manly Beacon to panoramic viewpoint

Natural Bridge 79
    Visit a large rock bridge, chutes and grottos

Coffin Peak 81
    Same panorama as Dante's View without the crowds

Dante's View 85
    Enjoy one of park's best vistas with visitors from around the world

Badwater 89
    Lowest point in North America

Panamint Valley & Panamint Range

PANAMINT DUNES ... 95
   Star-patterned sands beckon dune admirers

PANAMINT CITY ... 99
   Long hike to the ruins of "Pan a mint" City

DARWIN FALLS ... 103
   Surprising year-around creek, waterfall and mini-oasis

WILDROSE PEAK ... 107
   Charcoal kilns and marvelous hike in the middle of the Panamints

TELESCOPE PEAK ... 111
   Bristlecone pine-dotted national park high point (11,049 feet!)

DEATH VALLEY STORIES ... 114

CALIFORNIA'S NATIONAL PARKS ... 130

ABOUT THE AUTHOR ... 142

Golden Canyon: One of Death Valley National Park's most compelling hikes.

EVERY TRAIL TELLS A STORY.

Introduction

A bighorn sheep standing watch atop painted cliffs, sunlight and shadow playing atop the salt and soda floor, a blue-gray cascade of gravel pouring down a gorge to a land below the level of the sea—these are a few of the many awesome scenes I'll always remember from my hikes in Death Valley National Park.

Death Valley National *Park*? The Forty-niners, whose suffering gave the valley its name, would have howled at the notion. "Death Valley National Park" seems a contradiction in terms, an oxymoron of the great outdoors.

Park? Other four-letter words are more often associated with Death Valley: gold, mine, heat, lost, dead. And the four-letter words shouted by teamsters who drove the 20-mule team borax wagons across the valley floor need not be repeated.

Hike? Well, "hike" is a four-letter word not commonly associated with Death Valley. However, we who like to hike Death Valley intend to subvert the dominant paradigm and share the park's many intriguing trails.

"Death Valley" got its name from hikers—albeit unhappy ones. Looking for a shortcut to the California gold country, two groups of travelers with covered wagons got lost in the valley for weeks in December of 1849. After slaughtering their oxen and burning the wood of their wagons to cook the meat, they finally located a pass and hiked out of the valley. One of the pioneer women is reported to have said, "Goodbye Death Valley!" and the name stuck.

In Death Valley, where the forces of the earth are exposed to view with dramatic clarity: a sudden fault and a sink became a lake. The water evaporated, leaving behind borax and above all, fantastic scenery. Although Death Valley is called a valley, in actuality it is not. Valleys are carved by rivers. Death Valley is what geologists call a *graben*. Here a block of the earth's crust has dropped down along fault lines in relation to its mountain walls.

Death Graben National Park?

Nope. Just doesn't have the right ring to it.

Many of Death Valley's topographical features are associated with hellish images—Funeral Mountains, Furnace Creek, Dante's View, Coffin Peak and Devil's Golf Course—but the national park can be a place of great serenity for the hiker.

Introduction

At 3.4 million acres, Death Valley is the largest national park outside of Alaska. The very notion of Death Valley is a surprising one—even to some avid hikers. The desert that seems so huge when viewed from a car can seem even more intimidating on foot.

Compared to forest or mountain parks, Death Valley has a limited number of signed footpaths; nevertheless, hiking opportunities abound because roads (closed to vehicles), washes, and narrow canyons serve as excellent footpath substitutes.

The distances across Death Valley are enormous. If you only have one day, stick around the Furnace Creek Visitor Center. Take in Harmony Borax Works, Badwater, Dante's View and hike the interpretive trail through Golden Canyon.

Death Valley doesn't sound inviting, but the national park beckons hikers with an array of natural treasures accessible only on foot.

For the average hiker, there's a week or two's worth of hiking in the park, though you can get a fair sampling of this desert in three to four days. Although it's tempting, don't over-schedule. Death Valley is vast, with abundant sights to see and hikes to take.

To see as much of the park as possible, choose a different entrance and exit highway. Several routes lead into the park, all of which involve crossing one of the steep mountain ranges that isolate Death Valley from, well, everything. If you enter on Highway 127 through Death Valley Junction, exit on the scenic byway through the Panamint Valley. If you entered from the Panamint side, leave by following Badwater Road (Highway 178) south from Furnace Creek, across the Black Mountains and Greenwater Valley to intersect Highway 127 at Shoshone.

A particular highlight of hiking Death Valley is encountering the multitude of living things that have miraculously adapted to living in this land of little water, extreme heat and high winds. Two hundred species of birds are found in Death Valley. The brown whip-like stems of the creosote bush help shelter the movements of the kangaroo rat, desert tortoise and antelope ground squirrel. Night covers the movements of the bobcat, fox and coyote. Small bands of bighorn sheep roam remote slopes and peaks. Three species of desert pupfish, survivors from the Ice Age, are found in the valley's saline creeks and pools.

INTRODUCTION

In spring, even this most forbidding of deserts breaks into bloom. The deep blue pea-shaped flowers of the indigo bush brighten Daylight Pass. Lupine, paintbrush and Panamint daisies grow on the lower slopes of the Panamint Mountains while Mojave wildrose and mariposa lily dot the higher slopes.

In reality, Death Valley celebrates life. Despite the outward harshness of this land, when you take a hike and get to know the valley, you see it in a different light. As naturalist Joseph Wood Krutch put it: "Hardship looks attractive, scarcity becomes desirable, starkness takes on an unexpected beauty."

Hike smart, reconnect with nature and have a wonderful time on the trail.

Hike on.

—John McKinney

Gaze out at The Grandstand, an amazing rock monolith rising from Racetrack Playa.

EVERY TRAIL TELLS A STORY.

DEATH VALLEY

Geography

Located east of the Sierra Nevada and occupying a transition zone between the Great Basin and Mojave deserts, the park protects a diverse desert environment of mountains, valleys, canyons, badlands, salt dunes and salt flats.

Death Valley National Park is the largest national park in the lower contiguous 48 states. Some 91 percent of the park is official wilderness area.

At 282 feet below sea level, Badwater Basin on Death Valley's floor is the second-lowest point in the Western Hemisphere, and is located only 85 miles from Mt. Whitney (14,405 feet in elevation). This difference in elevation is the greatest elevation gradient in the contiguous United States. Highest peak in the park is 11,049-foot Telescope Peak at the top of the Panamint range.

Largely because of its lack of surface water and low relief, Death Valley is the hottest, driest place on the continent. The highest temperature in the world (134 °F) was recorded near Furnace Creek on July 10, 1913. Rainfall averages less than two inches a year and in some years no rain at all falls on Death Valley.

Natural History

Despite its bad rep as a desert wasteland, Death Valley is home and habitat for more than 1,000 species of plants and 440 species of animals that have adapted to extreme conditions. The park is an International Biosphere Reserve.

Only portions of the salt flats are devoid of plant life; the rest of the valley boasts at least some vegetation. More than two-dozen Death Valley plant species grow nowhere else on earth, including Death

Yawn. Hikers, keep an eye out for the park's wily—and sometimes sleepy—coyotes.

Valley sandpaper plant, Panamint locoweed, and napkin-ring buckwheat.

At lower elevations the dominant flora includes creosote bush and mesquite, plants that can extend their tap-root systems 50 feet to find groundwater. At higher elevations pinyon pine-juniper woodland thrive and limber pine and ancient bristlecone pine cling to life on the park's highest slopes.

Wildlife includes coyotes, rabbits, chipmunks, squirrels, the desert shrew, plus several species of gophers, rats and mice. Bats roost in caves, crevices and mine tunnels. Burros, introduced in the 1880s, roam the Panamint and Owlshead Mountains, as do the native mule deer. Desert bighorn sheep can be sighted in remote canyons and gamboling over inaccessible ridges.

Even the ubiquitous creosote looks lovely in bloom.

History

From as early at 7000 BC, Native American groups have lived in the region. About 1000 BC, the Timbisha (often referred to previously as the Shoshone) inhabited the area, migrating between the mountains in the summer and the valley in the winter. In 1849 a wagon train looking for a shortcut to California gave the valley its name, even though only one pioneer perished.

Many are the legends of Death Valley gold and silver mines, but the only truly profitable ore mined was borax, hauled out of the valley by the famed

"Death Valley Days" is by far the most successful syndicated television western series of all time.

twenty-mule teams. Radio programs and films helped Death Valley capture popular attention, and tourism began in earnest in the 1920s and accelerated in the 1930s when Death Valley National Monument was established and Depression-era government workers built facilities and hundreds of miles of good roads. Death Valley was substantially expanded and upgraded to national park status in 1994.

Administration

For camping, road and weather information call 760-786-3200 or visit nps.gov/deva. Furnace Creek Visitor Center & Museum, 15 miles inside the eastern park boundary on Calif. 190 (tel. 760/786-3200), offers interpretive exhibits and a new movie every half hour. Ask at the information desk for ranger-led nature walks and evening naturalist programs.

The park's nine campgrounds are at elevations ranging from below sea level to 8,000 feet. Make reservations online at http://reservations.nps.gov or call 877-444-6777.

Death Valley Natural History Association (dvnha.org) supports preservation efforts, interpretative programs, and scientific research. The group operates three book/gift stores in the park.

What looks like the road to nowhere leads somewhere special—the Eureka Dunes.

EVERY TRAIL TELLS A STORY.

I
Eureka Valley, Scotty's Castle & Racetrack Valley

HIKE ON.

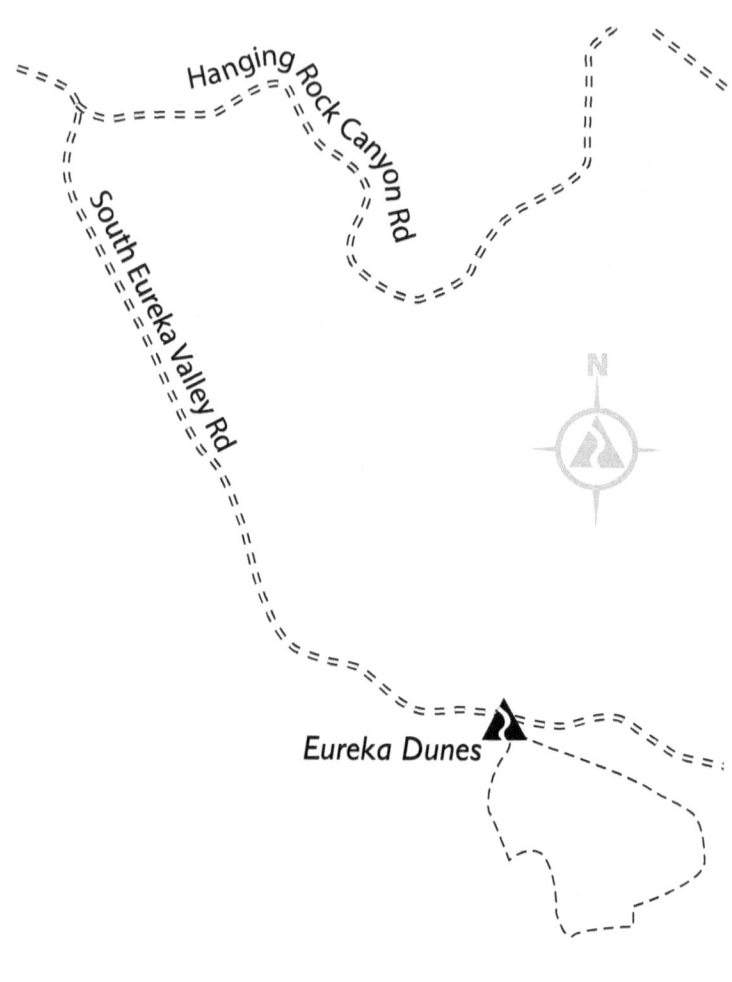

EUREKA DUNES

EUREKA DUNES TRAIL

1 to 5 miles round trip

Between the Owens Valley and Death Valley, isolated and often overlooked Eureka Valley holds many surprises, chief among them the Eureka Dunes. The dunes, formerly known as the Eureka Dunes National Natural Landmark and administered by the BLM, were added to the expanded Death Valley National Park in 1994.

The dunes occupy the site of an ancient lakebed, whose shoreline can be identified to the northeast of the dunes. The one-time flat lakebed northwest of the dunes sometimes captures a little surface water; this happenstance delights photographers who focus their cameras on the water and capture the reflection of the Saline Range or Last Chance Mountains.

The neighboring Last Chance Mountains gets a fair share of the meager rains that fall in these parts—meaning the dunes are (relatively) well watered. Rain percolates downward, the water later nurturing some 50 different dune plants even in the driest of years. Three species of flora occur nowhere else: Eureka dunes milkvetch, Eureka dune grass, and the showy, large white flowers of the Eureka Dunes evening primrose.

Like their cousins, the Kelso Dunes in Mojave National Preserve, the Eureka Dunes "boom." Low vibrational sounds are created when the wind-polished, well-rounded grains of sand slip-slide underfoot. The booming, which has been compared to a low-altitude airplane and a Tibetan gong, is audible but louder in the Kelso Dunes.

However, it's not the noise of Eureka Dunes, but the silence that impresses the hiker. The massive dunes (3.5 miles long and 0.5 mile wide) are California's highest at nearly 700 feet high.

DIRECTIONS: From the entrance station opposite Grapevine Campground, continue north on Scotty's Castle Road. The right fork leads to Scotty's Castle, but you continue toward Ubehebe Crater, 2.8 miles, then turn right onto dirt Big Pines/Death Valley Road. Drive some 21 miles northwest to Crankshaft Junction. Bear left, continuing on Big Pines/Death Valley Road which heads southwest up and over the Last Chance Range. (A few miles of the road through Hanging Rock Canyon are paved, the rest dirt.) After 12.3 miles, turn left (south) onto

South Eureka Road and travel 10.7 miles to the north end of the dunes and a road fork.

An ungraded road goes east to the north side (near interpretive signs) and primitive campsites. You can safely drive straight ahead to the northwest corner of the dunes. Respect the wilderness boundary and avoid getting stuck by staying on the established roads.

THE HIKE: The trail-less walking is strictly free-form up—and across—the dunes. If you get to the top of the island of sand, you'll get a unique vista of Eureka Valley and the many mountains that surround it: the Last Chance Range to the northeast, the Saline Range to the west, the Inyo Mountains to the southwest.

Sunrise over Eureka Dunes, California's highest.

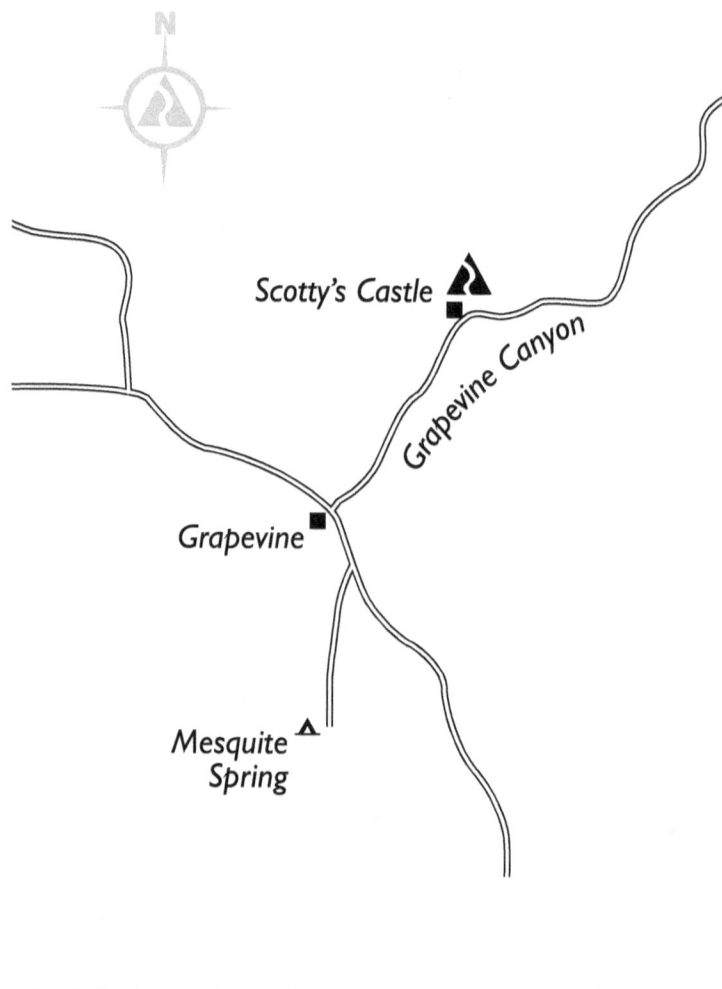

SCOTTY'S CASTLE
WINDY POINT TRAIL

From Castle to Scotty's grave is 0.75 mile round trip with 160-foot elevation gain

Scotty's Castle was shut down in October 2015 when flash floods damaged the ranch house, visitor center, and nearby roads. Check the NPS website for the latest information about the castle and scheduled tours.

Scotty's Castle, the Mediterranean-to-the-max mega-hacienda in the northern part of the park, is unabashedly Death Valley's premiere tourist attraction. Visitors are wowed by the elaborate Spanish tiles, well-crafted furnishings and innovative construction that included solar water heating. Even more compelling is the colorful history of this villa in remote Grapevine Canyon.

Construction of the "castle"—officially Death Valley Ranch—began in 1924. It was to be a winter retreat for eccentric Chicago millionaire Albert Johnson. The insurance tycoon's unlikely friendship with prospector-cowboy-spinner of tall tales Walter Scott put the $2.3 million structure on the map and captured the public's imagination. Scotty greeted visitors and told them fanciful stories from the early hard rock mining days of Death Valley.

The one-hour living history tour (fee) of Scotty's Castle is excellent, both for its inside look at the mansion and for what it reveals about the eccentricities of Johnson and Scotty. Tickets must be purchased in advance online or on the day of the tour, at the Scotty's Castle Visitor Center.

The National Park Service also offers specialty tours (reservations via phone or online; see above). Find out what's hidden under Scotty's Castle with The Underground Tour. Get into the basement and tunnel system to check out the historic technology—actually quite advanced for its time, as well as the high-tech methods the National Park Service is using to help preserve the Castle. To visit Scotty's Cabin (not castle) at Lower Vine Ranch, join a 2 ½-hour long ranger-guided hiking tour (2 miles round trip) over a graded dirt road.

Walk the castle grounds on your own (about 0.5 mile) from stable to swimming pool, from bunkhouse to powerhouse. Or take the short hike (0.75 mile round trip) through Tie Canyon Wash, which supplied sand and gravel for the castle's construction. Johnson bought 70 miles worth of abandoned railroad ties for firewood; thousands of them are still stacked in Tie Canyon.

Windy Point Trail offers great views of the castle and leads to a cross-marked grave.

DIRECTIONS: Scotty's Castle is located on Scotty's Castle Road, 53 miles from Furnace Creek. Take Highway north to Hwy 267 and turn right. Scotty's Castle will be on the left. Windy Point Trail begins just past the castle museum entrance.

THE HIKE: The path meanders around the bottom of a hill and soon offers views of the castle and its prominent clock tower. With the ascent come views of Tie Canyon, with its stacks of railroad ties and abandoned vehicles.

The trail curls around the hill to the summit. Windy Point is, indeed, often windy, but was actually named for Death Valley Scotty's dog who lies buried next to his master.

Hike Windy Point Trail for a great view of Scotty's Castle.

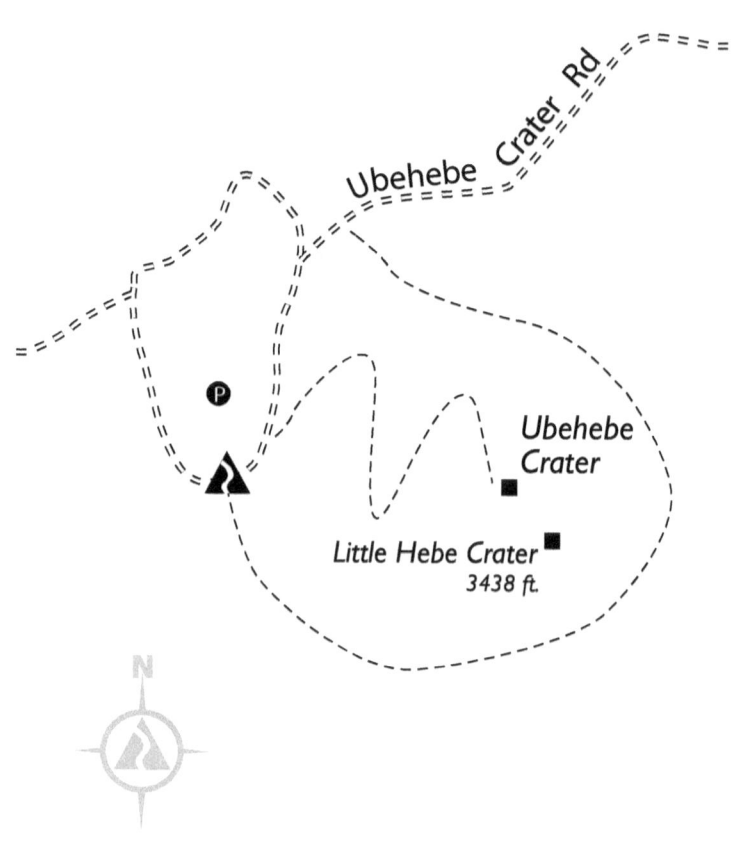

UBEHEBE CRATER

CRATER TRAIL

1.5 miles round trip with 200-foot elevation gain

Add volcanism to the list of cataclysms such as earthquakes and flash floods that caused high-speed changes to the Death Valley landscape. A short loop around Ubehebe Crater tours the cinder-covered rim of a volcanic crater and offer magnificent examples of volcanism.

Ubehebe (pronounced YOU-bee-HEE-bee) Crater, located at the north tip of the Cottonwood Mountains, is sometimes called an explosion craters. One look and you know why. Hot magma rose from the depths of the earth to meet ground water, with the resultant steam blasting out a crater and scattering cinders.

Ubehebe is thought to be the last and largest in a series of explosions that rocked the area. The hydro-volcanic (large steam explosions) eposides created pits known as maars. Little Hebe Crater, which grew in the middle of a large maar, is known as a spatter cone.

When measured by geological time, the crater is quite young. Ubehebe Crater, measuring about half mile in diameter from rim to rim, is believed to have been created about 1,000 years ago. It's explosion covered 6 square miles of desert with a layer of cinders 150 feet deep.

To the native Shoshone of Death Valley, the crater was known as *Temp-pin-tta Wo' sah*, "Basket in the Rock"—an apt description indeed. For an altogether different perspective on this part of Death Valley, scale Ubehebe Peak, located some 24 miles southwest of the crater. (See hike description.)

Ubehebe offers the hiker three short trails: a hike around the rim of the crater, a short trail to Little Hebe, and an optional descent to the bottom of the crater. Although many visitors are drawn to the rim of the Ubehebe, few descend to the bottom of the cinders.

Hold onto your hiker's hat! Winds at the rim of Ubehebe are often strong and can exceed 50 mph.

DIRECTIONS: From the Grapevine Ranger Station at the north end of the park, continue north (don't take the right fork to Scotty's Castle) 2.8 miles to the signed turnoff for Ubehebe Crater and continue another 2.5 miles to the crater parking area.

THE HIKE: From the edge of 500-to-777-foot deep Ubehebe Crater, join the south-trending path over loose cinders. The trail tops a couple of rises, then splits at a signed junction. Head south to Little Hebe. Walk the perimeter of the small crater and enjoy the views of the valley, and of the Last Chance Range to the west.

Return to Ubehebe Crater, note how much more eroded it is than younger Little Hebe, and resume passage around the rim. About 1.3 miles around the crater rim, intersect a path that descends into the crater. It's a 0.3 mile descent over volcanic cinders to the crater bottom; the ascent back to main trail and parking area is a bit of work because of the cinders slipping under your hiking boots.

Ubehebe is a unique hiking experience. It's not every day you get to walk around a volcanic crater.

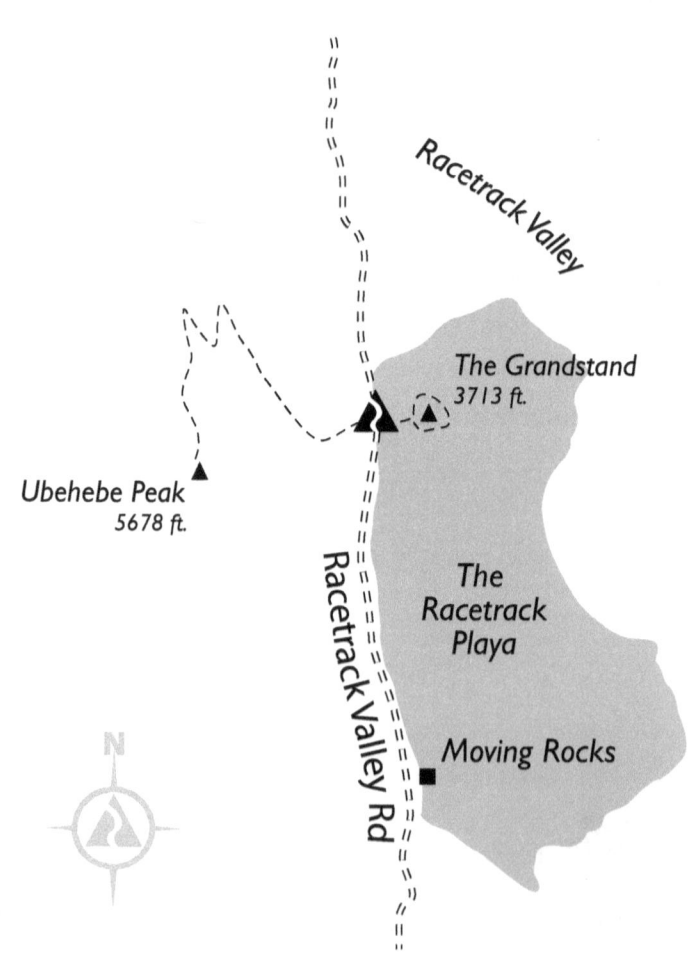

Ubehebe Peak

Ubehebe Peak Trail

To top of Ubehebe Peak is 6 miles round trip with 2,000-foot gain

Marvelous vistas are the hiker's reward for climbing the steep trail to Ubehebe Peak, a remote summit in the equally remote Last Chance Range. The White Mountains, Saline Valley and High Sierra peaks are among the sights to be seen from the peak.

Ubehebe means "Big Basket" in the Shoshone language; such a name seems more appropriate to Ubehebe Crater some 24 miles northeast of the rocky peak.

For most travelers, the attraction in this part of the park is not rarely visited Ubehebe Peak but the three-mile long mud flat known as the Racetrack. Rocks are pushed along the sometimes muddy surface by high winds, leaving long faint tracks. Most of the tracks you're likely to see on the playa are made by smaller rocks, but throughout the years there have been reports of rocks weighing several hundred pounds skidding for a quarter mile.

The Grandstand, a rock outcropping at the northern end of the Racetrack is an easy half-mile hike from the pullout off Racetrack Valley Road. This pullout is also the trailhead for the hike to Ubehebe Peak.

The old miners' trail that leads to the crest is in fairly good condition. To reach the very top of Ubehebe Peak, though, requires some rock scrambling (Class 2-3); however, traveling only as far as the crest delivers equally good views.

DIRECTIONS: From the Grapevine Ranger Station at the north end of the park, continue north (don't take the right fork to Scotty's Castle) 2.8 miles to the signed turnoff for Ubehebe Crater and continue another 2.5 miles. The paved road ends with a left turn into the Ubehebe Crater parking lot, but you continue south some 20 miles on the washboard-surfaced, occasionally rough Racetrack Valley Road to Tea Kettle Junction, colorfully decorated with tea kettles. Bear right, traveling another 5.7 miles to a turnout on the right (west) side of the road opposite the Grandstand and the Racetrack. The trail to Ubehebe Peak heads west from the parking area.

THE HIKE: The path begins a moderate ascent through a creosote-dotted alluvial fan and after a half mile steepens and begins a series of switchbacks, climbing higher over the desert-varnished shoulder of the peak. Many a switchback brings you to the north ridge of the peak, about 1.8 miles from the trailhead.

Stay left at a fork in the trail and continue the steep ascent for another half mile, curving around to the west side of the peak. The path drops 0.2 mile to a saddle at the 2.6 miles mark, where the trail ends.

If you want to bag the peak, climb southward along a cairn-marked route, carefully picking your way around steep rock faces then rock scrambling up to the small summit area atop 5,678-foot Ubehebe Peak. Savor the panorama: the Inyo Mountains, the Racetrack, the Cottonwood Mountains, Telescope Peak and the snow-capped peaks of the High Sierra.

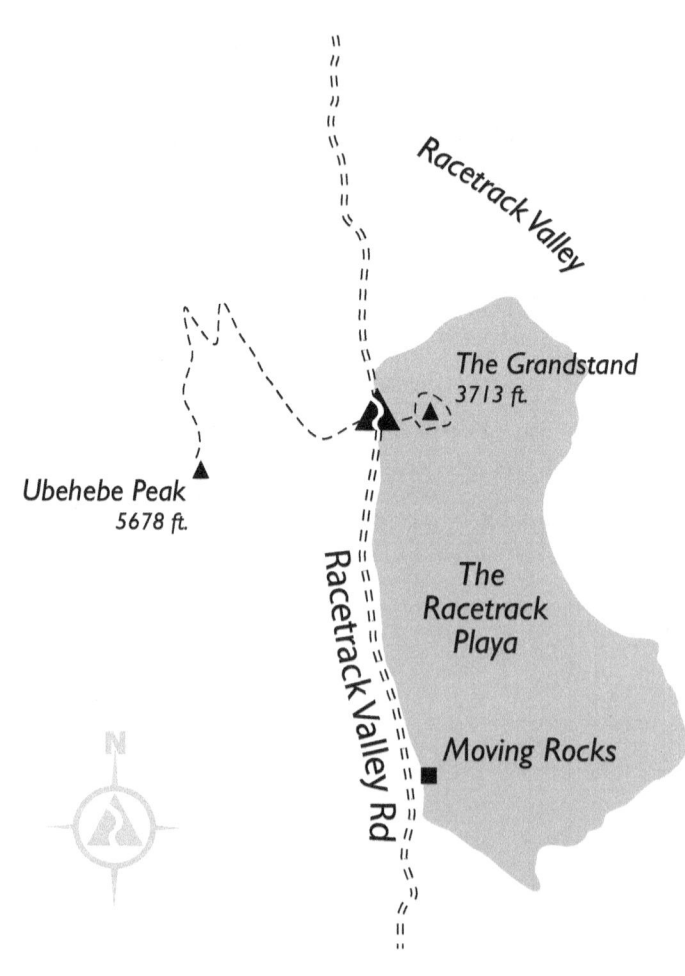

Racetrack Valley

Racetrack Valley Trail

To Sliding Rocks is 1 to 2 miles round trip

The amazing sliding rocks scooting across Racetrack Valley may be the national park's weirdest phenomena of all. Geologists have been unable to determine exactly how rocks migrate around the Racetrack.

An ancient lakebed, the Racetrack is a 2.5-mile long, oval-shaped dry mud flat. A rock outcropping at the north end of the Racetrack is known as The Grandstand.

Rocks of various sizes (baseball to basketball) slide across the old lakebed leaving tracks in their wake. These tracks (about six inches wide or so, depending on the size of the rock) are straight, curved and even looped, and extend as much as 600 feet.

Nineteenth-century prospectors noticed the sliding rocks and earth scientists have studied them since the 1950s. Scientists have measured the rocks' location change, but no one has ever seen the rocks actually move.

Scientists theorize that the rocks slide after rain moistens the top couple centimeters of the lake bed and a high wind (perhaps 70 miles per hour or more) arises to push them around the track. Other theories suppose that accumulated rain water forms ice when night temperatures fall below freezing and wind drives these floating ice sheets. These theories do not explain why the rocks move in such peculiar patterns. Some rocks have made sudden right-angle turns, others have made complete loops and ended up almost exactly where they began.

The sliding rocks are not one of Death Valley's roadside attractions and a long drive and a short hike (a mile or two) are necessary in order to visit them. Even if you're not fortunate enough to be the first human to observe the rocks move, you'll have a great time tracing the rock tracks and playing on the playa.

DIRECTIONS: From Furnace Creek Visitor Center, drive 17 miles north on Highway 190, then bear right on the road to Scotty's Castle and proceed 32 more miles to the Grapevine Ranger Station and entry kiosk. Head north toward Ubehebe Crater for 5 miles.

The paved road ends with a left turn into the Ubehebe Crater parking lot, but you continue south 20 miles on the washboard-surface, occasionally rough dirt Racetrack Valley Road (suitable for high-clearance vehicles equipped with light truck tires; standard passenger car tires are susceptible to flats on this road) to

Tea Kettle Junction, colorfully decorated with teakettles. Bear right, and travel another 6 miles to The Grandstand on the left side of the road and 2 more miles to parking for the Racetrack.

THE HIKE: Head due east across the old lakebed. Hiking straight across the valley is the quickest and most direct route to the rocks, though walking in other directions will also eventually deliver you to the rocks in due time.

A half-mile of hiking brings you to the first rock tracks. If you keep hiking toward the mountains on the far side of the lakebed you'll encounter more and more rocks and accompanying tracks. (These mountains supply the sliding rocks.)

Wander at will among the rocks and return the way you came.

A long drive and short hike leads to close-up views of the mysterious Sliding Rocks.

A trailless scramble leads to the top of Death Valley Buttes, a trio of hills. Great views!

EVERY TRAIL TELLS A STORY.

II
Stovepipe Wells and Beyond

HIKE ON.

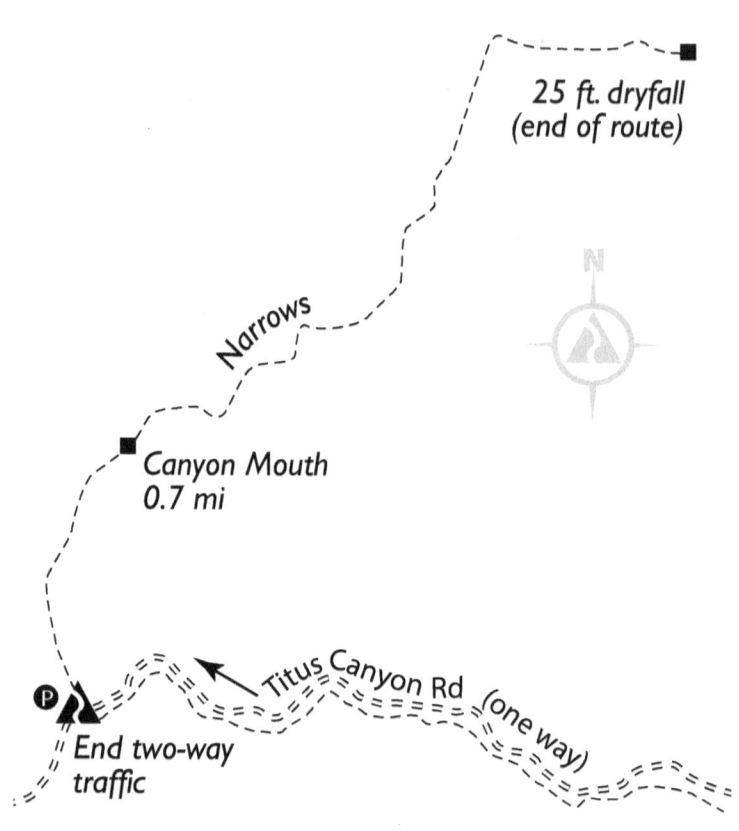

TITUS CANYON
TITUS CANYON TRAIL

Through narrow part of canyon is 4 miles round trip; to Klare Spring is 12 miles round trip

In Titus Canyon, gray and white cliffs, red and green hills, and fractured and contorted rocks point to the tremendous geologic forces that shaped the land we call Death Valley.

Hikers can explore a twisting narrows, where a block of the earth's crust has dropped down along fault lines in relation to its mountain walls.

The canyon is named for Morris Titus who, in 1906, left the Nevada boomtown of Rhyolite (now a historic ghost town) with a prospecting party. When the prospectors were camped in the canyon, water supplies dwindled. Titus left in search of water and help, but was never seen again.

Winding through the canyon is 27-mile long Titus Canyon Road, a narrow, one-way dirt road. (NPS recommends high clearance vehicles;

four-wheel drive may be necessary in adverse weather/road conditions.)

In theory vehicles and hikers should not be sharing a narrow thoroughfare; in practice the arrangement works OK. Those motorists who brave Titus Canyon tend to be a courteous lot and hikers can hear vehicles from a long way off, thus avoiding potential mishaps. It's best to hike before 11 a.m. when almost no vehicles are present.

The road was constructed to reach Leadfield, which boomed in 1925 due to the slick efforts of a promoter who controlled a very low-grade deposit of lead ore. Soon a town was built in the narrow canyon; its population swelled to 300. A year later, the town was empty. Today only a shack or two and some crumbling foundations mark Leadfield, but the road that serviced the mines and miners remains behind, beckoning to those who prospect for scenery.

DIRECTIONS: The lower part of Titus Canyon Road is two-way and leads to the trailhead. From its junction with Highway 190, drive north on the road toward Scotty's Castle 14.3 miles to the turnoff for Titus Canyon. Follow Titus Canyon Road 2.7 miles east to a parking area at the mouth of Titus Canyon. (To reach the start of one-way Titus Canyon Road: From Highway 190, a few miles from Stovepipe Wells, head northeast on Daylight Pass Road toward Beatty, Nevada, some 25 miles away. About 4 miles short of Beatty is the signed turnoff for Titus Canyon.)

THE HIKE: It's moderate uphill walking along the gravel floor of the canyon. Marvel at the awesome folding and faulting of the canyon's rock walls. The Narrows is only 20 feet wide in places. For a moderate walk through the rock show, continue about 2 miles up-canyon and turn around when the narrow canyon widens.

More gung-ho hikers will keep trekking up Titus Canyon, which widens a bit. Nearly six miles out is Klare Spring, a waterhole occasionally visited by a band of bighorn sheep. Observe, but don't touch the ancient petroglyphs.

Just beyond the spring is a wildly contorted section of canyon wall. Try to determine just which end of the rock formation is up, then head back down Titus Canyon to the trailhead.

Sure you can drive through it, but it's lots more memorable to hike Titus Canyon.

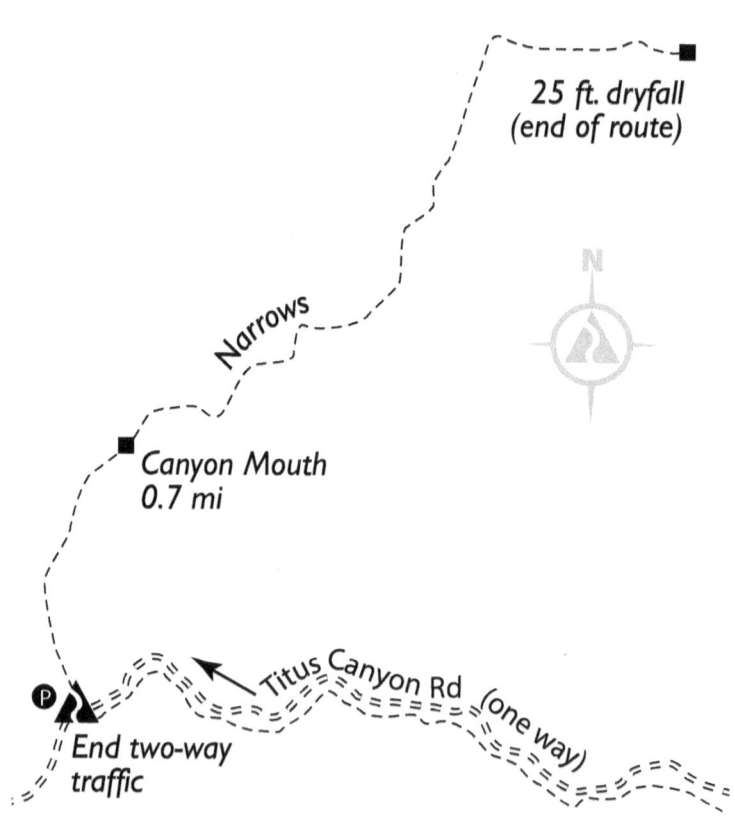

Fall Canyon

Fall Canyon Trail

To Narrows is 6.5 miles round trip with 1,100-foot elevation gain

Hike through a dramatic gash in the Grapevine Mountains among soaring walls and the polished rock of a narrows. With its colorful, contorted rock walls, Fall Canyon ranks among the most magnificent canyons in the park. Depending on the angle of the sun and what it illuminates, the canyon's rock displays hues of red, brown, sepia and umber.

Fall Canyon shares a trailhead with Titus Canyon, one of Death Valley's marquee canyons, but also one accessible to vehicles. In the eyes of many hikers, a roadless canyon is automatically more revered than one open to vehicle travel; thus Fall Canyon will rate higher than far better known Titus Canyon.

Fall Canyon is growing in popularity, but you might just find some solitude in its narrow passageways. The canyon floor is the loose soil of a wash and thus can be slow-going.

Fall Canyon gets its name from a 20-foot high dry waterfall located 3 miles up the canyon. Sure-footed hikers can circumvent the fall with a bit of rock scrambling and by way of short use trail along the canyon wall. The fall bypass route should be undertaken only by experienced hikers. A dramatic segment of canyon lies on the other side of the dry fall.

DIRECTIONS: The lower part of Titus Canyon Road is two-way and leads to the trailhead. From its junction with Highway 190, drive north on the road toward Scotty's Castle 14.3 miles to the turnoff for Titus Canyon. Follow Titus Canyon Road 2.7 miles east to a parking area at the mouth of Titus Canyon.

THE HIKE: From the parking area, head north on an unsigned path (don't trek into Titus Canyon). The trail dips and rises, traveling over low ridges and into shallow washes until it reaches the main Fall Canyon Wash a bit more than 0.5 mile from the trailhead.

Not long after you probe the mouth of the canyon, the trail fades away and the canyon walls, from a hiker's point of view, seems to vault higher and higher. At 1.3 miles, the canyon walls narrow to about 20 feet.

Gaze upward at the colorful walls and continue as the canyon widens then narrows again at the 2.5-mile mark. This particular narrows is so narrow that the canyon floor is in nearly perpetual shade—a welcome respite on a hot afternoon.

Three miles out, stand face to rock face with the high dry fall. To bypass the fall, retrace your steps 300 feet or so down the wash and look for rock cairns on the canyon's south wall. Carefully ascend the short rock pitch up to the use trail that continues along the canyon wall to the right of the fall.

Just beyond the fall the canyon is a very narrow world of polished rock. You can wander 0.3 mile or so farther through the rock passageway—a dramatic conclusion to this splendid hike.

Into the Fall Canyon Narrows—so narrow, in fact, it shuts out sunlight, and is one of the shadiest spots in the park.

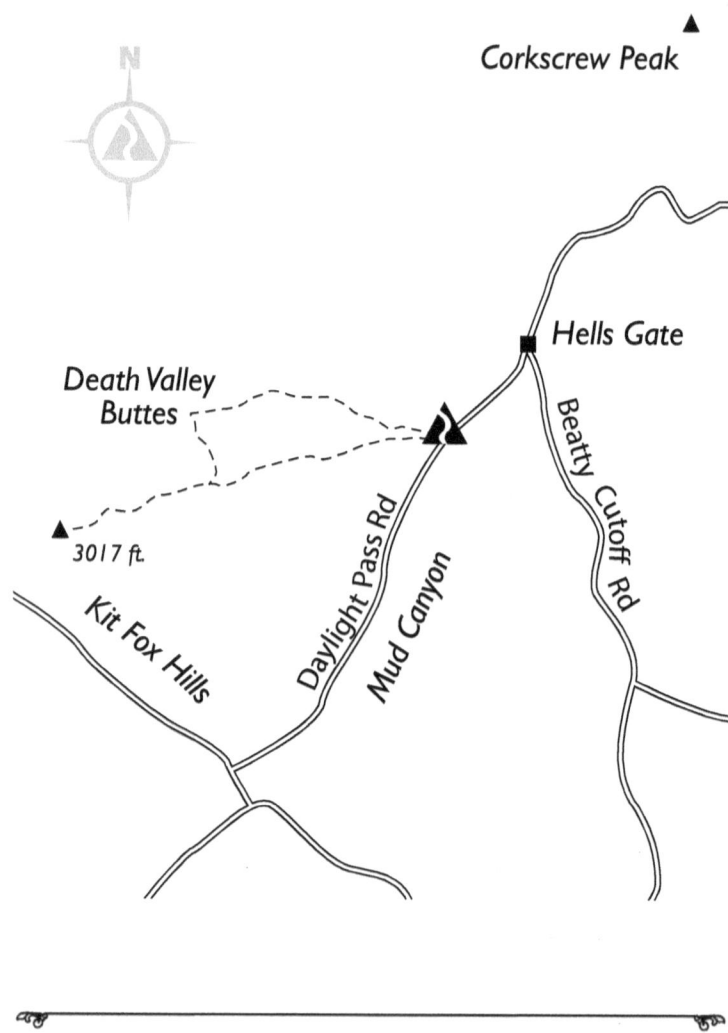

DEATH VALLEY BUTTES

DEATH VALLEY BUTTES TRAIL

From Hells Gate to the top of the buttes is 4 miles round trip with 900-foot elevation gain

Grand views of the central part of the national park are the hiker's reward for a trail-less scramble to the top of Death Valley Buttes, three distinct hills at the base of the Grapevine Mountains. The sweeping panorama includes the valley floor, the Funeral and Panamint ranges.

Erosion of the range left much rock debris at the base of the mountains; this alluvium gradually buried lower ridges, leaving behind isolated high points of which the most prominent are the Death Valley Buttes.

The route to the buttes begins at Hells Gate—named, as the story goes, in 1905 by a teamster who was struck by the contrast between the relative cool of Boundary Canyon and the hotter area near buttes. The mules would act startled and shake their heads at the sudden searing heat. "They thought they had stuck their noses through the gates of hell," the teamster is reported to have exclaimed.

Hells Gate may seem an unlikely place in which to build a resort, but that's just what Bob Eichbaum dreamed of doing in the 1920s. In 1905, the young electrical engineer became enchanted with Death Valley when he helped construct an electrical plant in Rhyolite. After 20 years in the tourist business in Venice Beach and on Catalina Island, he returned to Death Valley intent on building a grand hotel, what he termed "one of the wonders of the country." He planned to collect customers in Los Angeles and bus them to Hells Gate, but bad roads doomed his plan and his resort was never built. (Eichbaum, however, did open the original Stovepipe Wells Hotel in 1926, as well as the Eichbaum Toll Road over Townes Pass into the valley.)

The cross-country route to the buttes is easy enough to accomplish. More difficult is the narrow, rocky ridge that must be traversed—best left to experienced hikers.

DIRECTIONS: From the Furnace Creek Visitor Center, head north on Highway 190 for eleven miles. Veer right toward Beatty on the Daylight Pass Cutoff and travel northeast ten miles to Hells Gate, where you'll find a large parking area and picnic tables.

THE HIKE: Walk southwest toward the buttes across rocky terrain dotted with creosote and beavertail cactus. Look for the remains of the phone line that crossed this land, connecting Rhyolite to civilization, such as it was, in the southwest.

After 0.5 mile, leave behind this relatively gentle alluvial fan and strike south toward the ridge of the easternmost butte. Follow the rock crest westward, aided by an intermittent trail, to the 2,725-foot summit. Admire the barren Grapevine Mountains nearby, and the equally austere Funeral Mountains extending southeast.

Return the way you came or continue to the next and highest butte. If you press on (only for experienced hikers), you'll descend the steep ridgeline west to a saddle, then ascend the narrow ridge 0.5 mile to Peak 3,017. Enjoy the view across the shimmering valley floor to the Panamint Mountains.

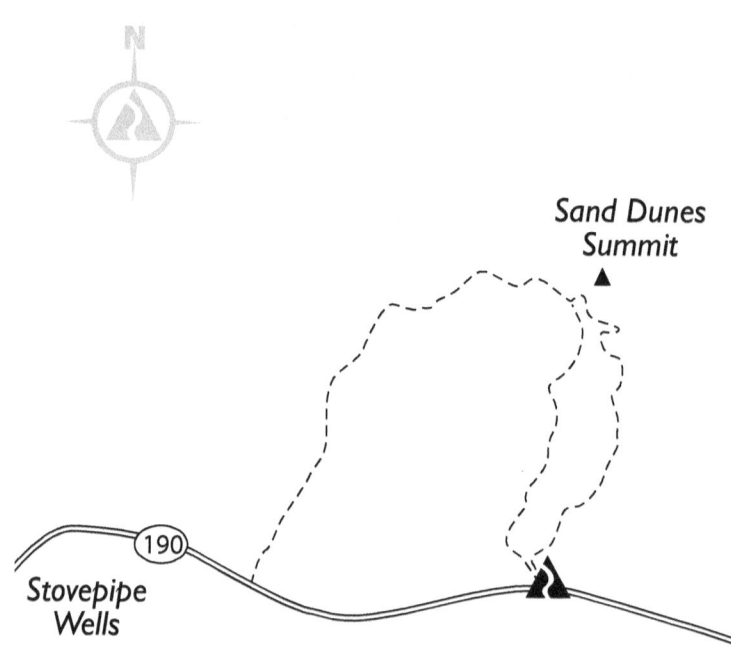

Mesquite Flat Dunes

Dunes Trail

From 2 to 4 miles round trip

A 14-square mile field of dunes and bizarre geology are some of the attractions of hiking around the Stovepipe Wells area of Death Valley National Park.

Mesquite Flat Dunes, Death Valley's most visible, best known and easiest to access dunes, lie between Towne Pass on the west and Daylight Pass to the east; there's quite a sand-laden draft between the two passes. The 14-square mile field of dunes has long been a favorite of park visitors and of filmmakers who have used the handsome sand piles in many movies, including films in the Star Wars series.

While extensive, the dunes aren't very high. Star Dune, highest in the complex, stands about 130 feet or so depending on the wind; this is low compared to other dunes in the park with sand depths of more than 600 feet.

Hiking the dunes is most fun in the cooler morning and late afternoon hours. At these hours, the dunes are at their most photogenic, too; the light is softer, the shadows longer.

Death Valley's dunes are formed in much the same way as those mega-dunes in the Middle East or North Africa. What nature needs to form dunes is fairly simple: a source of sand, wind to separate the sand from gravel, more wind to roll the sand along into drifts, and still more wind, perhaps in the form of a backdraft, to keep the dunes in place. Supplying sand to the Mesquite Flat Dunes are the Cottonwood Mountains, located to the north and northwest of the dunes.

As you hike the dunes, notice blow sand (loose, very fine particles) piled on the leeward side of plants; these piles are known as sand shadows. Stands of creosote bush and the occasional mesquite cling to life on the dunes.

The Mesquite Flat Dunes system includes three types of dunes: star-shaped, linear and crescent-shaped. The sand dunes are actually tiny pieces of rock, most of them fragments of quartz and feldspar.

Near the dunes are some weird natural features. Those surrealistic-looking corn stalks you see across Highway 190 from the dunes are actually clumps of arrow-weed. The Devil's Cornstalks are perched on wind- and water-eroded pedestals.

Fringing the dunes are expanses of dry mud that have cracked and buckled into interesting patterns. These mud sink areas and the edges of the dunes themselves are good places to look for the tracks of the few desert creatures able to survive in the harsh environment—most notably rabbits and kangaroo rats.

DIRECTIONS: Take Highway 190 to the signed turnoff for the dunes located 2 miles east of Stovepipe Wells. Turn right into the parking lot.

THE HIKE: Your hike into the dunes is exactly what you make of it—short or long, a direct or indirect route to the higher sand formations. Figure 4 miles max to climb up, down and around the taller dunes and return.

Remember that doing the dunes means a two-steps-forward-one-step-backward kind of hiking, so pace yourself accordingly. Wear shoes; sand surfaces can be very hot.

Take an (easy) hike to Mesquite Flat Dunes, Death Valley's best-known dunes.

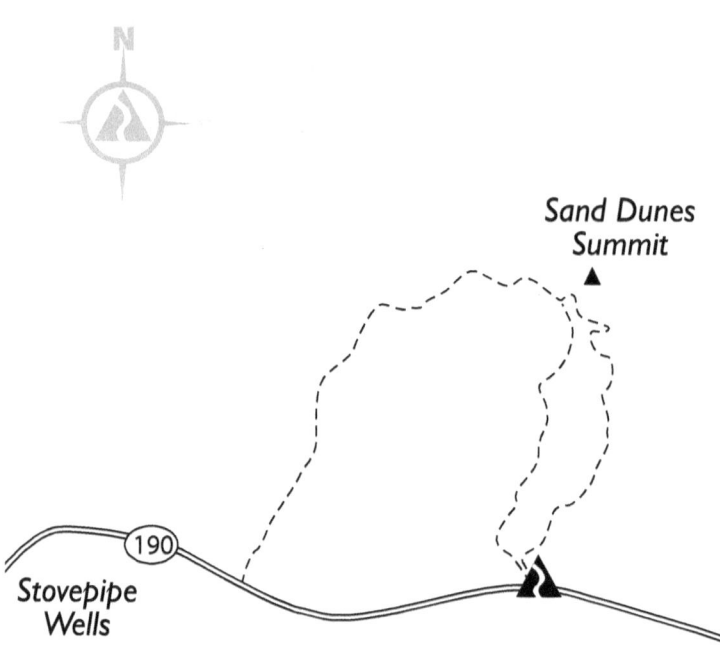

Mosaic Canyon

Mosaic Canyon Trail

4 miles round trip

Some Death Valley canyons deliver the scenery promised in their names: Golden, Red Wall, and Corkscrew, to name a few.

Mosaic Canyon is another fine example of truth-in-labeling. The canyon, located near Stovepipe Wells, displays mosaics of water polished white, gray and black rock.

Nature has cemented the canyon's stream gravels into mosaics large and small. It's easy to imagine you've entered an art gallery when you view the mosaics on the canyon walls; not only are nature's works of art on display, but the long and narrow white marble walls of the canyon seem quite "gallery"-like.

Mosaic is one of those desert canyons that's hourglass in shape: a fairly wide head and mouth, with a narrow deep gorge in between. This shape means that during a storm, rainwater collects on the broad surface area at the head of the canyon then funnels through the narrow canyon midsection at high velocity. The water, laden with rock debris, sculpts the canyon into its photogenic form, and polishes the rock walls.

(By the way, a narrow canyon like Mosaic is the very last place you want to be in a rainstorm!)

Mosaic Canyon is an ideal family outing. Rangers lead interpretive walks through the canyon. Check at the main park visitor center in Furnace Creek or the small center at Stovepipe Wells for schedules of guided walks.

Serious hikers can persevere several more miles up ever-steeper slopes toward the head of Mosaic Canyon or enjoy the rock-climbing challenge afforded by rugged tributary canyons.

DIRECTIONS: From the west end of Stovepipe Wells village, turn south on the signed dirt road for Mosaic Canyon. Follow the bumpy road (suitable for passenger cars with good ground clearance) 2.5 miles to its end at a parking lot.

THE HIKE: Walk up the sand and gravel canyon bottom. In a short time, you'll round a bend and enter a corridor of polished rock. Within the first 0.25 mile, marvel at the marble surfaces that have long made Mosaic a visitor favorite.

At the next bend you'll climb a dry waterfall. The farther you go, the higher the walls get, exposing more and more of the mosaics that gave the canyon its name.

After 0.75 mile, the canyon opens up into a wider wash. As you hike along, marveling at the mosaics, a couple of minor canyons join Mosaic on your right. These can be explored if you have the inclination and determination.

As the wash narrows again at a dry fall, a steep marble chute a bit less than two miles from the trailhead marks the end of the trail. This is a good turnaround point; stop while you're having a good time and before you exceed your abilities.

This can be a fun return trip. Kids like sliding down the short water chutes and everyone likes the fine vistas of Death Valley.

Admire the mosaics in the "gallery" of Mosaic Canyon.

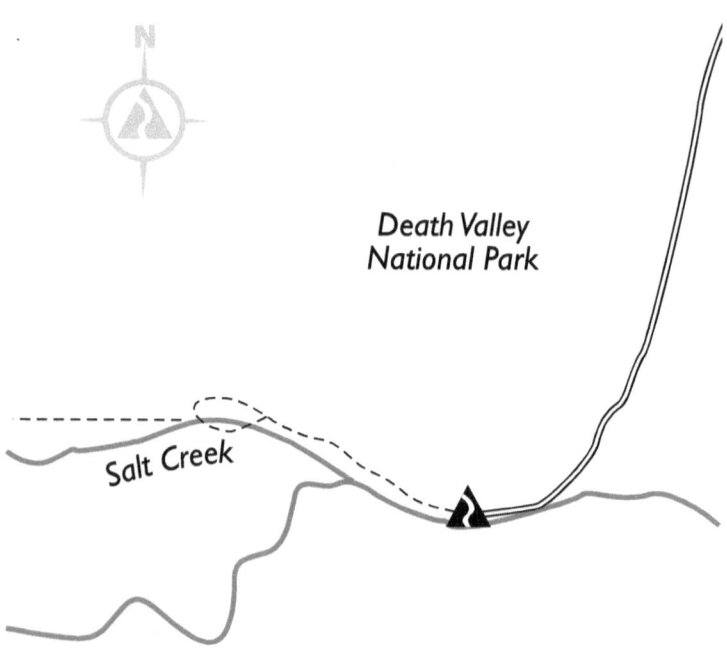

SALT CREEK

SALT CREEK INTERPRETIVE TRAIL

0.5 mile loop; longer options possible

Salt Creek is the home of the Salt Creek pupfish, found nowhere else on earth. A nature trail along a boardwalk tells the amazing story of *Cyprinodron Salinus*.

Many desert creatures display unusual adaptation to the rigors of life in arid lands and changes in their environment, but few have had to make more remarkable adjustments than the little Salt Creek pupfish.

Thousands of years ago a large freshwater lake covered the area. Gradually this lake shrunk smaller and smaller while the lake's salinity greatly increased. Many plants and animals failed to adapt to an environment radically different from the one in which their forebears existed.

But the pupfish adapted—evolved the ability to filter salt water, remove the excess salt and excrete it through kidneys or gills. And the inch-long fish, used to a lot of water and a fairly constant temperature, adapted to life in a relatively tiny amount of water that varies in temperature from near freezing to nearly 100 degrees.

Once the pupfish were so numerous that the valley's native peoples harvested them for food. They were still numerous when the *1938 WPA Guide to Death Valley* described them: "Prospectors amuse themselves by holding a pan full of crumbs just below the surface and watching the greedy fish crowd in to eat. They come so rapidly and in such numbers, that they sometimes make small waves."

The pupfish population is protected by a park service-built boardwalk that reduces the impact of visitors on the soft creek banks.

Best months to see the fish are from February to mid-April. In spring a million pupfish might be wriggling in the creek; by the end of spring, a few thousand remain.

Those hikers familiar with California's coastal trails might be reminded of one of those nature trails around an estuary: a boardwalk path lined with pickleweed and salt grass, plenty of interpretive signs, plus the tangy scent of saltwater.

DIRECTIONS: From Highway 190, some 13 miles north of Furnace Creek, turn west on Salt Creek Road and follow it 1.2 miles to the parking area.

THE HIKE: Walk the boardwalk, which extends along the creek. At creek-crossings, you get up-close views at the pupfish.

At the northern end of the loop, leave the boardwalk and take the footpath continuing north along the east side of the creek. Walk another 0.5 mile or so along the nearly 2-mile long creek. You'll see more pupfish, as well as birds ranging from snipes to great blue herons.

Hike along Salt Creek, home of the Salt Creek pupfish that has miraculously adapted to life in this ultra-hostile environment.

Makes you wonder where all that water came from to sculpt Natural Bridge.

EVERY TRAIL TELLS A STORY.

III
Furnace Creek & Amargosa Range

HIKE ON.

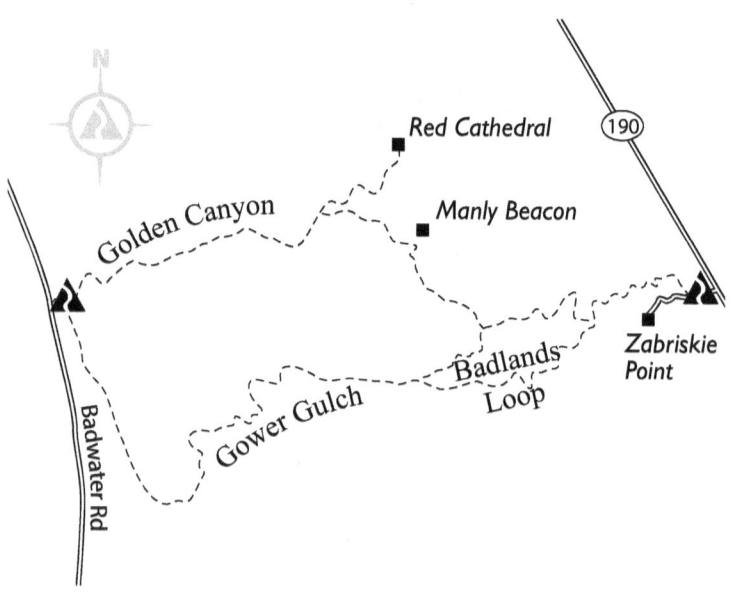

Golden Canyon

From Golden Canyon Trailhead to Red Cathedral is 2.8 miles round trip

The panoramic view of Golden Canyon from Zabriskie Point is magnificent, but don't miss getting right into the canyon itself—only possible by hitting the trail. Sunrise and sunset, when the light is magical and fellow hikers are very few, are particularly good times to hike an excellent interpretive trail through the canyon.

Until the rainy winter of 1976, a road extended into Golden Canyon. A desert deluge washed away the road, and it's been a trail ever since.

The first mile of Golden Canyon Trail is a self-guided interpretive trail. You may learn more about Miocene volcanic activity, Jurassic granitic intrusion and Precambrian erosion than you ever wanted to know; nevertheless, even the most casual student of earth science will gain an appreciation for the complex geology and the millions of years required to sculpt and color Golden Canyon. Aptly named Red Cathedral looms over the canyon in colorful contrast.

DIRECTIONS: From the Furnace Creek Visitor Center, drive south on Highway 190, forking right onto Badwater Road. The signed Golden Canyon Trail is on your left, three miles from the visitor center. The hike through Golden Canyon shares a common trailhead with the longer excursion to Zabriskie Point.

THE HIKE: From the parking lot, hike up the alluvial fan into the canyon. Depending on the light, Golden Canyon can seem to glow gold, brass, yellow or orange.

Marvel at the tilted, faulted rock walls of the canyon as they close in around you. Notice the ripple marks, created long ago by water lapping at the shore of an ancient lake. Early into your tour, look for a number of narrow side canyons well worth an exploration.

Deeper and deeper into the badlands you ascend. Watch for white crystalline outcroppings of gypsum—similar to but not the same stuff of 20 Mule Team fame. "White gold," Death Valley prospectors, called it. Not exactly a glamorous substance, but a profitable one.

A mile from the trailhead, at the end of the nature trail, the path branches. One fork (0.4 mile one way) heads for Red Cathedral, also called Red Cliffs.

Golden Canyon

Reach it by continuing up the main canyon over broken pavement to the old Golden Canyon parking lot.

The trail narrows and you continue by squeezing past boulders to the base of Red Cathedral, a colorful natural amphitheater. The red color is essentially iron oxide—rust—produced by weathering of rocks with a high iron content. It's all the more dramatic because the red rock caps yellow-gold formations. Gaze out at Telescope Peak on the far, far horizon. Return the same way or by a longer route through Gower Gulch (see description in this guide.)

Hike highlight: the trail across the Badlands between Golden Canyon and Gower Gulch.

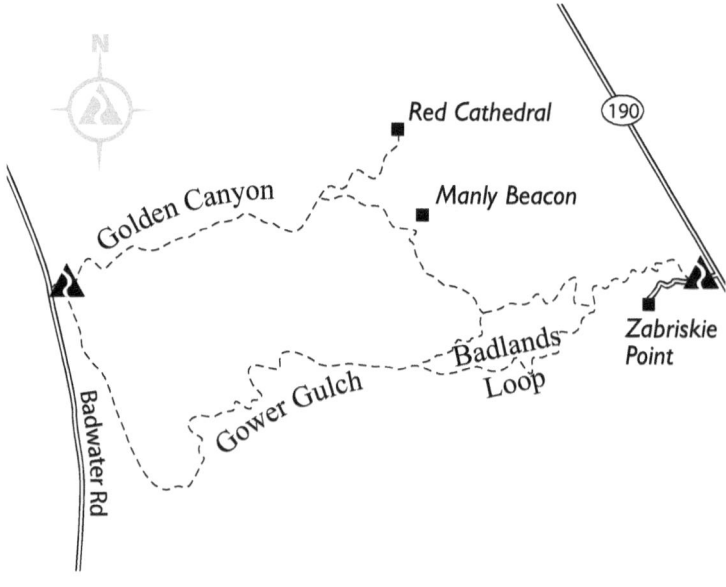

Zabriskie Point and Gower Gulch

To Zabriskie Point with return via Gower Gulch is 6.5 miles round trip with 900-foot elevation gain

While it's true you can drive to Zabriskie Point, you'll appreciate the view much more by sweating up those switchbacks on foot. The memorable panorama from Zabriskie Point includes a grand view of the valley, framed by the badlands just below and the Panamint Mountains to the west.

An engaging trail climbs through badlands to the point named for Christian Brevoort Zabriskie, one of the early heads of Death Valley borax mining operations. A return by way of Gower Gulch offers another perspective on this colorful desert land and enables hikers to make a loop.

DIRECTIONS: From the Furnace Creek Visitor Center, drive south on Highway 190, forking right onto Badwater Road. The signed Golden Canyon Trail is on your left, 3 miles from the visitor center.

The hike to Zabriskie Point shares a common trailhead with the shorter excursion through Golden Canyon.

THE HIKE: Follow the Golden Canyon Interpretive Trail (see description in this guide) for one mile to stop 10 and take the signed fork toward Zabriskie Point. The path climbs into the badlands toward Manly Beacon, a pinnacle of gold sandstone. The trail crests at the shoulder of the beacon, then descends into the badlands and brings you to a junction 2.5 miles from the trailhead.

Go left (east) to Zabriskie Point. (The right fork is the return leg of your loop through Gower Gulch.)

Watch for Park Service signs to stay on the trail, which is a bit difficult to follow as it marches up and down the severely eroded silt-stone hills. After a mile, a final steep grade brings you to Zabriskie Point—or, more accurately, the parking lot.

Step uphill to the point itself, and savor the vast views of the eroded yellow hills below and the mountains across the valley.

Before sunrise, photographers set up their tripods at Zabriskie Point and point their cameras down at the pale mudstone hills of Golden Canyon and the great valley beyond. The display of color from purple to gold as sun passes over Golden Canyon is memorable to say the least.

Zabriskie Point and Gower Gulch

Retrace your steps back to the trail fork.

This time you'll descend west into a wash. Wide, gray and gravelly Gower Gulch has definitely felt the hand of man. The open mouths of tunnels and white smears on the gulch walls are reminders of the borax miners who dug up these hills. Gower Gulch has been altered considerably in order to protect Furnace Creek developments from flooding.

A bit more than a mile down the trail, the gulch narrows and you'll suddenly encounter a 30-foot-high dry fall. Take the bypass footpath to the right. A final 1.2 mile of trail heads north along the base of the hills, on a route paralleling the highway, and leads back to the trailhead parking area at the mouth of Golden Canyon.

From Zabriskie Point, eye-popping views of the Red Cliffs.

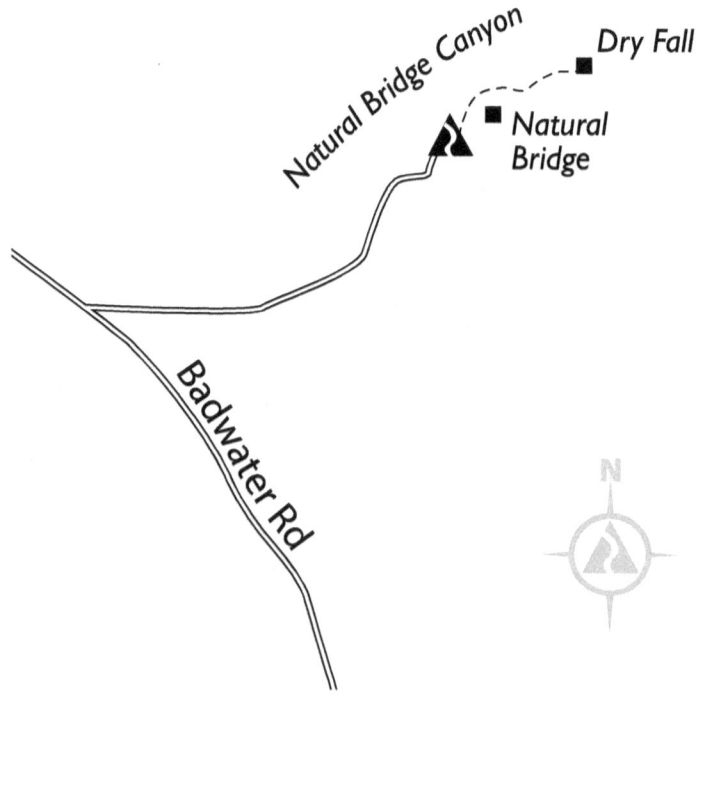

Natural Bridge

Natural Bridge Trail

To Natural Bridge is 0.8 mile round trip

Long ago, water surged through a canyon wall, stripping away weaker strata and leaving behind a 50-foot high rock bridge spanning the canyon. Beyond the bridge, explore other water-cut formations—grottoes, benches, chutes and spillways.

DIRECTIONS: From Badwater Road, 15 miles south of Furnace Creek Visitors Center, follow the signed dirt road 1.5 miles to the Natural Bridge trailhead.

THE HIKE: Head up the gravel-floored canyon bottom. Before long, the volcanic walls of the canyon narrow and you'll meet up with the natural bridge. To extend this sojourn, walk under the bridge and continue up-canyon. A dry waterfall, about 0.75 mile from the trailhead can be surmounted, but the 20-foot-high dry fall a mile out halts this hike.

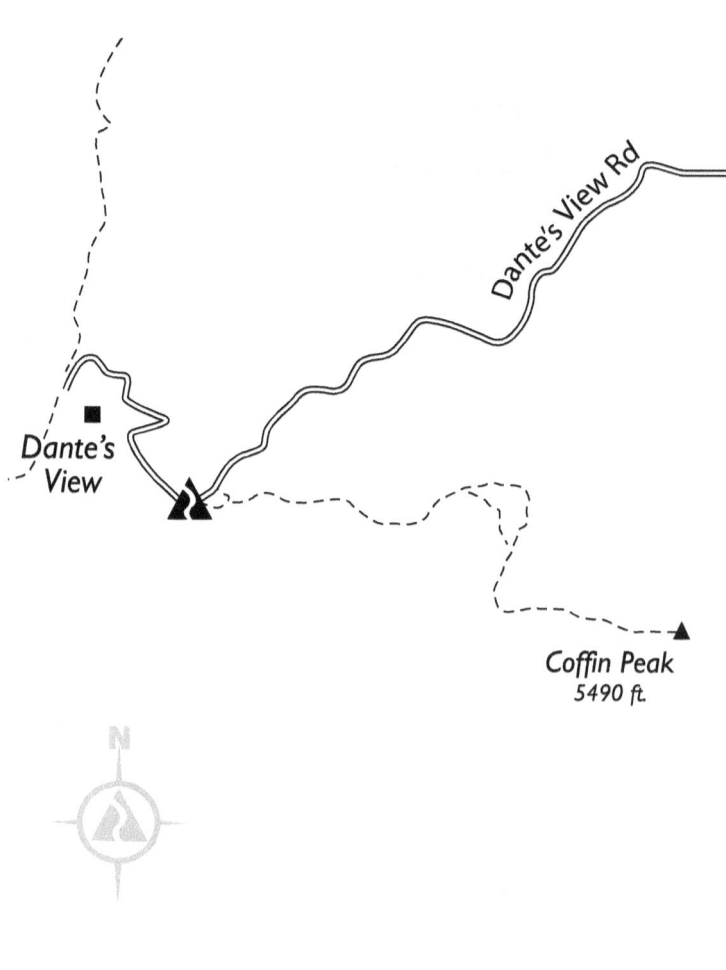

COFFIN PEAK

COFFIN PEAK TRAIL

From picnic area below Dante's View to Coffin Peak is 2.5 miles with 300-foot elevation gain

Make no mistake: Dante's View offers one of Death Valley's finest panoramas. Trouble is, you can drive to the viewpoint—and thousands of motorists do, meaning your chances for quiet contemplation of the desert below are about as slim as the possibility of rainfall.

For the hiker, there is an alternative: Coffin Peak, offering the same great view as Dante's without the crowds. The 5,503-foot peak (a smidgen higher than 5,475-foot Dante's View) is situated in the relatively little-traveled Black Mountains that extend along the southeastern boundary of the national park.

From atop Coffin Peak unfolds a panorama never to be forgotten. A vertical mile down lies the lowest spot on the continent. Opposite the peak, across Death Valley, rise Telescope Peak and the snow-clad summits of the Panamints. Farther still, on the western horizon, loom the granite ramparts of the Sierra Nevada. North and south from Coffin Peak is the Funeral Range. And from here, too, is the glimmer of that alkaline pool called Badwater—or is that just a mirage?

In addition to Dante's View, the other major visitor attraction in the Black Mountains is Greenwater, where a few ruins and building foundations are all that remain of a copper mining boomtown. The hype after the 1905 discovery of copper attracted a thousand people and soon Greenwater had stores, saloons, a post office, and even two newspapers and a men's magazine. What Greenwater lacked, however, was quality ore, and by 1908 Greenwater was a ghost town.

Hikers experienced with cross-country travel will be most comfortable with the trail-less trek to Coffin Peak; however, the less experienced can set out with the assurance that this hike for the most part stays within sight of Dante's View Road.

DIRECTIONS: From Badwater Road, Highway 190 junction just south of the Furnace Creek Visitor Center, drive 10.8 miles on Highway 190 toward Death Valley Junction. Turn right on Dante's View Road and continue 12.6 miles (0.6 mile short of Dante's View). Turn left and park in a turnout with a restroom.

THE HIKE: From the picnic site, hike east, parallel to Dante's View Road, ascending a hill dotted with Mormon tea. Dodging spiny shrubs, follow the ridgecrest as it bends southeast and climbs to the top of a 5,360-foot hill.

Continue east among handsome desert varnish-stained boulders, savoring the valley views. Top another hill, descend northeastward to a saddle, then climb to Peak 5484.

Now follow the crest south, then east, toward the conical summit of Coffin Peak. Your view encompasses the Black Mountains, south and north, the Funeral Mountains to the northeast, and the Greenwater Valley, green indeed with creosote, to the southeast. The shimmering valley floor backed by the high Panamint Mountains to the west, completes the panoramic view.

Well, not quite. Just to the northwest is Dante's View, usually swarming with sightseers.

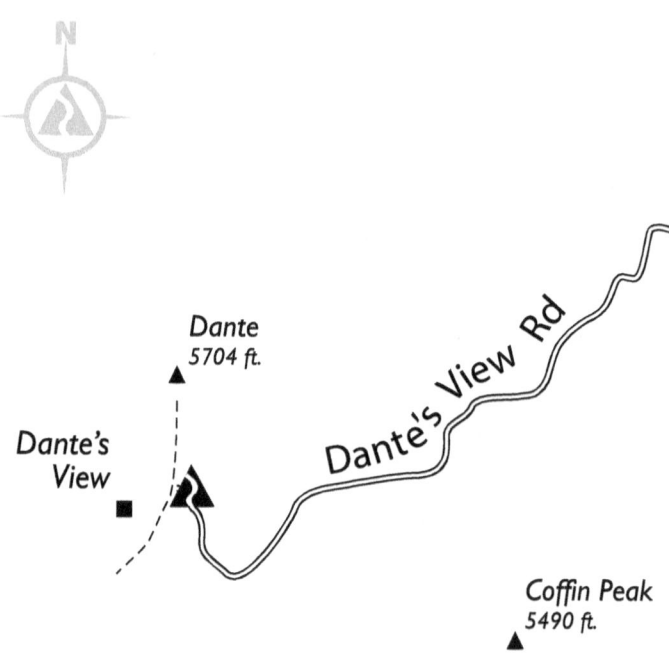

Dante's Peak

Dante's View Trail

To Dante's Peak and beyond is 1 mile round trip with 200-foot elevation gain

The short hike toward Dante's Peak, perched more than a mile above the valley floor, offers grand vistas of the lowest and highest points in the continental U.S. Beyond Badwater towers 11,049-foot Telescope Peak and farther still, 14,494-foot Mt. Whitney.

From the parking area, an unsigned, but distinct trail leaves the tourists behind and ascends north toward Dante's Point. A second unsigned little trail (0.25 mile) extends southwest from the parking area to a rocky promontory popular with photographers.

Hellish names to the contrary, Death Valley, as surveyed from Dante's View, appears far from lifeless. The dark splotches on the Panamint Mountains are actually bristlecone pine, pinyon and juniper. Those small dark spots observed along the west side of the valley are mesquite thickets.

Directly below Dante's is the vast salt sink. The gleaming white beds of almost pure salt contrast with the brown, gray, tan and taupe elsewhere on the valley floor.

Dante's View was created during Death Valley's pre-park days in the 1920s. Local innkeeper Charlie Brown escorted a group of private tour operators high into the Black Mountains to partake of what he considered the best view. All agreed that tourists would be wowed by such vistas—the vast valley, Badwater and Mount Whitney.

Brown was soon awarded a contract to construct a road to the viewpoint and within a few months "Dante's View," as it was dubbed, became the first stop on the Union Pacific's Death Valley bus tours.

"Dante's View," the 1998 movie, was a thriller starring Sheryl Lee as a cold-blooded jewel thief on the run who meets up with an innocent Death Valley gal when her truck overheats in the searing heart of the valley.

Take the hike in the early morning hours so the sun is at your back when you're savoring the view or photographing the inspirational scene. Dante's View even offers great views at night—of the stars with a telescope.

Consider taking a light jacket; temperatures at Dante's View average some 25 degrees less than those on the valley floor.

DIRECTIONS: From Highway 190, 12 miles east of Furnace Creek, turn south on Dante's View Road and follow it 13.2 miles to its end at Dante's View parking area.

THE HIKE: Read the interpretive signs at the edge of the overlook, enjoy the view, then walk north along the road 0.1 mile and join the unsigned footpath leading toward Dante's Peak. The trail climbs briskly and briefly up a hill, and then makes a mellow contour along the mountain's west slope. About 0.3 mile from the trailhead, the path meets the summit ridge, then ascends a bit more to reach Dante's Peak.

Ascend Dante's Peak for far-reaching valley views.

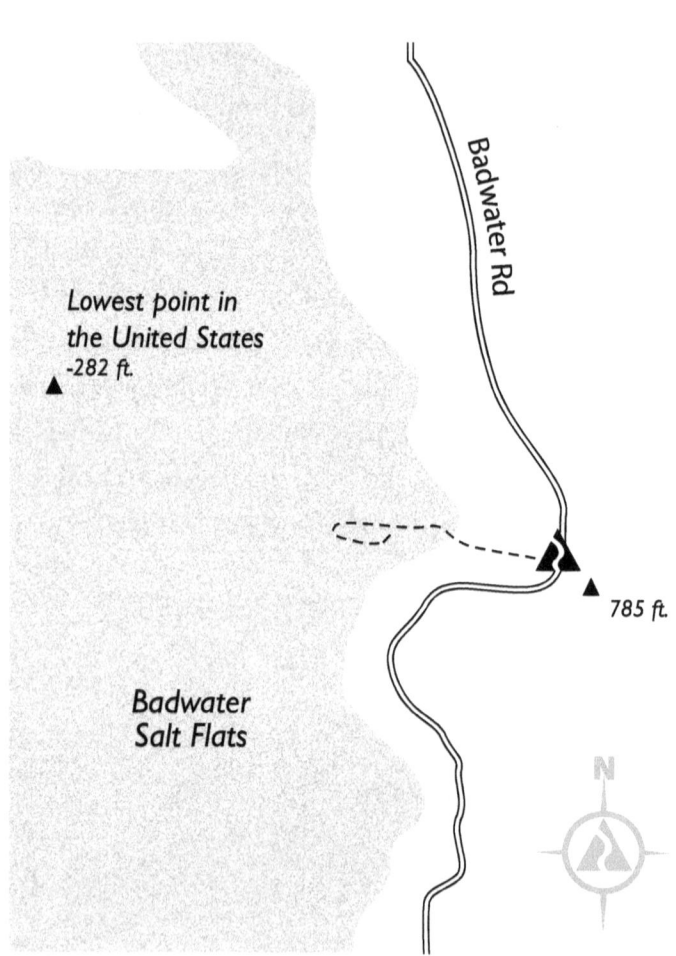

TheTrailmaster.com

BADWATER

BADWATER TRAIL

From Badwater Road onto Salt Flats is 1 mile round trip

Looking west from Badwater, the lowest point in North America at 282 feet below sea level, the eye is drawn to what appears to be a shallow stream flowing across the valley floor. But this flow is a mirage caused by the strange terrain and deceptive colorings.

Light plays upon the valley floor, and the mind spins as though caught in a color wheel, from the gray and gold of sunrise to the lavender and purple of sunset. To say the least, visiting the lowest parts of Death Valley is often a colorful experience.

Badwater—and some of the nearby canyons off Badwater Road—offer object lessons of Death Valley geology in action, as well as shifting patterns of light and iridescent colors that makes hikes in this part of the national park ones to remember.

A hike across the barren salt flats to Badwater and beyond may just be the definitive Death Valley experience. It's an excursion into extremes—the lowest land in North America and one of the hottest places on earth. Because temperature increases as elevation decreases, Badwater is no place to linger in the summer when temperatures of 120 degrees F. are regularly recorded.

Speaking of extremes, the 135-mile Badwater Ultramarathon, promoted as "the world's toughest footrace," begins at Badwater and ends at Whitney Portal (elevation 8,360 feet), trailhead for Mt. Whitney.

While Badwater is not the planet's lowest land (that distinction belongs to the Dead Sea, located some 1,290 feet below sea level in Israel), its proximity to adjacent high country makes its lowness seem quite pronounced. National Park highpoint Telescope Peak (11,048 feet) is located fewer than 20 miles west of Badwater.

As the story goes, an early mapmaker named the briny pools "Badwater" when his mule refused to partake of the water. Badwater's water is indeed bad—as is most surface water in Death Valley—because of an extremely high concentration of salts; undrinkable it is, but not poisonous.

While Badwater's environmental conditions are hostile to life, some plants and animals manage to survive. Salt grass and clumps of pickleweed edge the shallow pools, where water beetles and the larvae of insects can be observed.

DIRECTIONS: From the junction of Highways 190 and Badwater Road, head south on the latter for 16.5 miles to the signed Badwater parking area on the west side of the road.

THE HIKE: From the parking lot, gaze up at a "Sea Level" sign posted high on the cliffs above Badwater; it helps you imagine just what a depression 282 feet represents. These cliffs thrust skyward all the way up to Dante's View, 5,775 feet above sea level.

A causeway leads out onto the salt flats. To really get a feel for the enormity of the valley floor, continue past the well-beaten pathway farther out onto the salt flats.

A surreal scene at Badwater, lowest elevation in the U.S.

Be sure to check out the curious beehive-shaped Wildrose Charcoal Kilns that date from the 1870s.

EVERY TRAIL TELLS A STORY.

IV
Panamint Valley & Panamint Range

HIKE ON.

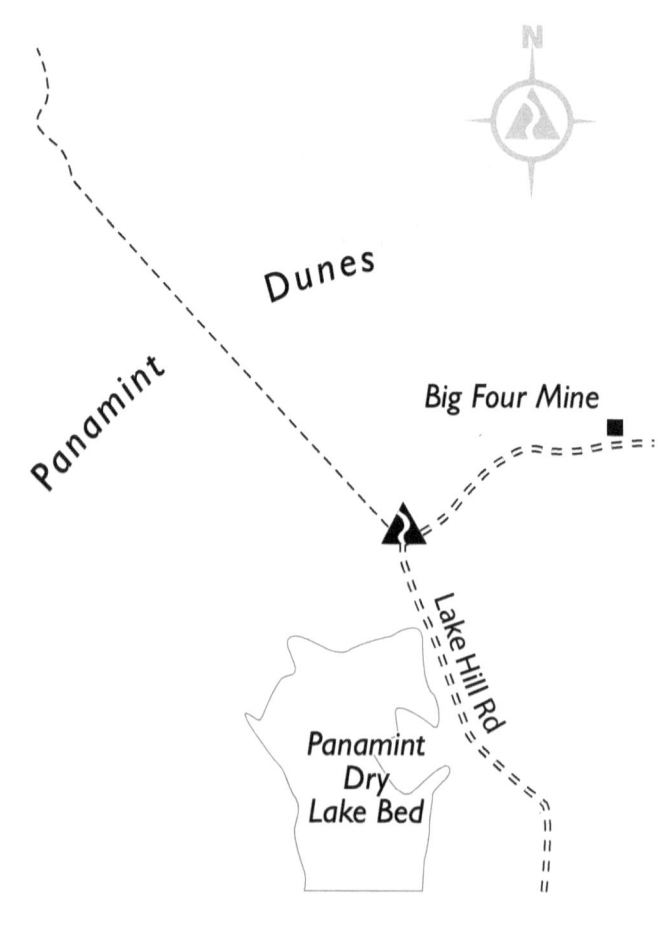

Panamint Dunes
Dunes Cross-country Route

To top of highest dunes is 9 miles round trip with 1,100-foot elevation gain

They're not the California Desert's highest, longest or largest, but the Panamint Dunes are often adjudged the most pristine by dune connoisseurs. This pristine quality is likely one of the happy results of this dune complex's lack of easy access.

Surrounded by the Cottonwood, Nelson and Panamint mountain ranges, the dunes not only feel remote but are remote—four miles from the nearest road. (If you want dunes close to a road, head over to the Mesquite Flat Sand Dunes near Stovepipe Wells.)

The dunes look easy to access from the trailhead; however, a 4-mile ascent over the desert floor is required just to reach the base of the most attractive taller dunes.

After reaching the top of this inspiring sandscape, most hikers think their effort time well spent. The

Panamint Dunes are star-shaped and in the right light hikers might conclude they've captured a fallen star.

The Panamints, like dune ecosystems elsewhere, appear devoid of life, but actually offer habitat for a number of plants and animals. The most obviously successful flora is dune grass, which thrives on the north side of the dunes. Look for the tacks of such denizens of the dunes as the Mojave fringe-toed lizard, the kangaroo rat and kit fox.

DIRECTIONS: From Highway 190 at Panamint Springs, head 5 miles east to unsigned Lake Hill Road. Turn north and travel 5.7 miles on the rough gravel road (suitable for passenger cars with high ground clearance). When the road begins to swing steeply right (bending northeast), look for a small parking area and the trailhead. But don't block the road; it continues as a four-wheel drive-only route.

THE HIKE: From the parking area, take aim at the dunes and begin hiking across a rock strewn alluvial fan which, fortunately for the feet, soon gives way to compacted sand. Some 2.5 miles of trail-less tramping over the sand brings you to the very base of the dunes.

Keeping company with creosote bushes, you ascend onward, your progress slowed by softer sand. After another mile-plus of slow walking, you'll gain the lower edges of the highest dunes. Look behind you occasionally to keep your bearing in relation to the trailhead so you'll be better able to navigate on your return.

Improvise an upward trajectory over the ridges and around the hollows of the ever-changing dunes. Gain the rather narrow dune ridge line and savor the panorama.

From atop the dunes, the vista is a dreamy one of the heat-shimmering Panamint Valley extending far south, the bordering Cottonwood Mountains to the east, colorful Panamint Butte to the southeast and civilization in the form of Panamint Springs to the southwest.

Pay particular attention to Telescope Peak to the far southeast. If you navigate straight toward the peak on your return route, you'll be on a fairly accurate course back to the trailhead.

Well worth the extra effort to reach Panamint Dunes.

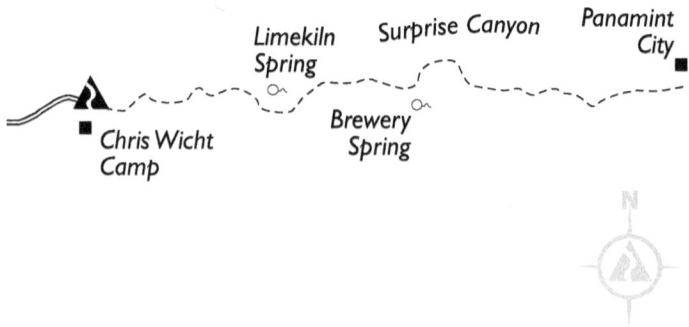

Panamint City

Surprise Canyon Trail

From Chris Wicht Camp to Panamint City is 11 miles round trip with 3,200-foot elevation gain

"Pan a mint," was the cry of prospectors who swarmed into these mountains after silver was discovered in 1873. By 1875 once tranquil Surprise Canyon was the locale of Panamint City boasting a population of 2,000.

With a multitude of saloons, a house of ill fame in Little Chief Canyon, a Boot Hill in Sourdough Canyon, and a very high homicide rate, the town had a reputation nearly as bad as Bodie. To its credit, however, Panamint City also had a newspaper—Death Valley's first.

Much of the ore was reduced right in Panamint by the company's huge twenty-stamp mill, built of a half-million bricks and, by one account, "the closest thing to a church Panamint ever had."

Nature's fickleness (ore veins were hard to work and did not live up to initial promise) and nature's fury ended mining operations. A 1901 flash flood washed away the remains of Panamint City, long after it was deserted. Mining attempts over the next 100 years all failed.

The former road, now a footpath, leads to Panamint City, where its glory days are recalled by stone foundations and the ore smelter's tall brick chimney. Mid-20th century mining artifacts include buildings, machinery trucks and trailers.

The brushy route frequently crosses the creek in the lower canyon as it probes a very rough, rocky and (surprisingly wet) narrows. Springs trickle down canyon walls and feed the year-around creek in Surprise Canyon.

A variety of environments from bare cliffs to barrel cactus, from willow groves to juniper woodland, add surprises to the canyon trek. Hikers might spot burros or bighorn sheep gamboling high on the canyon walls.

DIRECTIONS: From Highway 190, some 34 miles west of Stovepipe Wells and just 2.5 miles east of the hamlet of Panamint Springs, head south on Panamint Valley Road for 14 miles to Trona-Wildrose Road. Turn south (right) and proceed 9.5 miles to Ballarat Road. Turn left and head 3.5 miles into tiny Ballarat. Turn north on Indian Canyon Road and travel 2 miles to Surprise Canyon Road, turn right and continue 4 miles to road's end. Park alongside the road next to the primitive campground.

THE HIKE: The path (washed-out road) meanders creekside with occasional crossings through sometimes narrow, sometimes wide, Surprise Canyon. Early on, the trail establishes a pattern that continues for 3.5 wet miles.

Finally, the route leaves the creek behind and begins an aggressive 1.5 miles of ascent. After gaining a thousand feet in elevation, glimpse the first of Panamint City's far-flung mining ruins about 5 miles from the trailhead.

The road emerges from the narrows and reaches the head of Surprise Canyon, a bowl surrounded by pinyon pine-dotted slopes.

This is a hard hike: bushwhacking through thick brush, hiking in the creek, a killer climb. A very long 5.5 miles to reach the first stop—a cabin known as the Panamint Hilton.

Only ruins (circa 1875 and mid-20th century) remain of silver mine boomtown Panamint City.

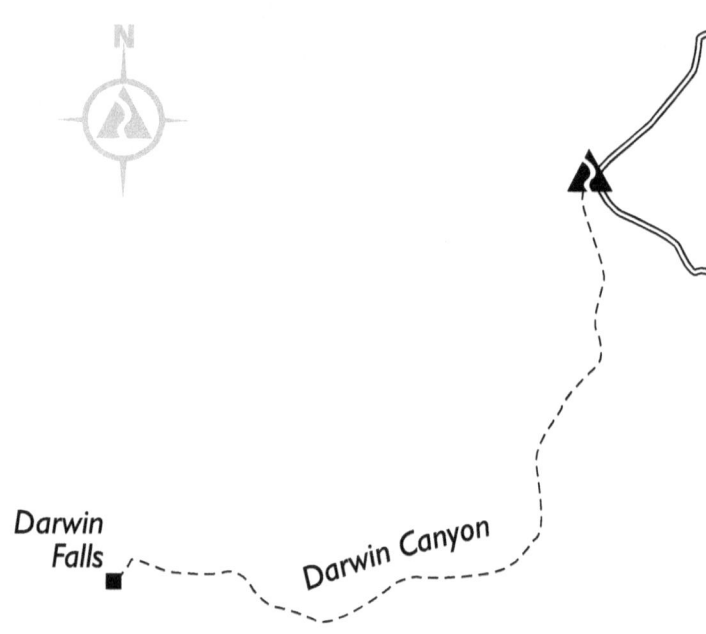

DARWIN FALLS

DARWIN FALLS TRAIL

To Darwin Falls is 2 miles round trip

Tucked away in (what appears to be) a forlorn range of mountains on the east side of the Panamint Valley is a year-around creek and waterfall. Darwin Falls and the mini-oasis surrounding it are small reminders of the surprises found off the main Mojave roads.

When Congress passed the landmark California Desert Protection Act of 1994, Death Valley National Park gained considerable acreage on its western frontier, including Darwin Falls, once a centerpiece of a BLM wilderness study area. It's well worth a stop, particularly for the visitor entering the park from the west via U.S. Highway 395 and California State Highway 190.

Darwin Falls is fed by an underground spring bubbling to the surface of the volcanic rock floor of Darwin Canyon. Wildlife and more than eighty species of birds find water and shelter at the cottonwood and willow-fringed oasis.

During the 19th century boomtown days of Darwin, a Chinese-American farmer grew vegetables in a rich patch of earth below the falls and sold his produce to the miners. "China Garden Springs" is still on the map.

In the 2011 feature-length documentary film, "Darwin," filmmaker Nick Brandestini introduces us to an interesting cast of characters living in the near-ghost town of Darwin on the edge of Death Valley.

The desolate desert outpost thrived during various mining eras in the 19th and 20th centuries with the population at one time reaching 3,500 residents. Now Darwin counts just 35 inhabitants, in a place lacking any church or children, government or economy.

Along with a multitude of internal struggles, the denizens of Darwin also face external threats—an antiquated water system and their town's close proximity to a military bombing range. And yet they are an enduring lot, who say there's no place like home—even if that home is in Darwin, a town full of ramshackle buildings, rusted vehicles and abandoned mining equipment located at the end of the road to nowhere.

Best time for a visit to Darwin Falls are the cooler months, and in spring when the creek flow is the greatest, the falls at their fullest. Plan on getting your boots wet with numerous creek crossings and look forward to a swim and picnic at the base of the Darwin Falls.

DIRECTIONS: From Highway 190, one mile west of tiny Panamint Springs, turn southwest on an unsigned gravel road. Drive 2.5 miles on the rough road and turn right into the trailhead parking area.

THE HIKE: It's dry-going when you first walk the canyon bottom, but after a half mile or so the canyon narrows and you'll begin walking alongside a little creek. The final quarter mile of travel requires numerous creek crossings.

Behold the 20-foot Darwin Falls and a unique scene in Death Valley National Park. More cascades are located above the falls but be careful if you decide on further exploration.

Is this really Death Valley? Hike to a mini-oasis and spring-fed Darwin Falls.

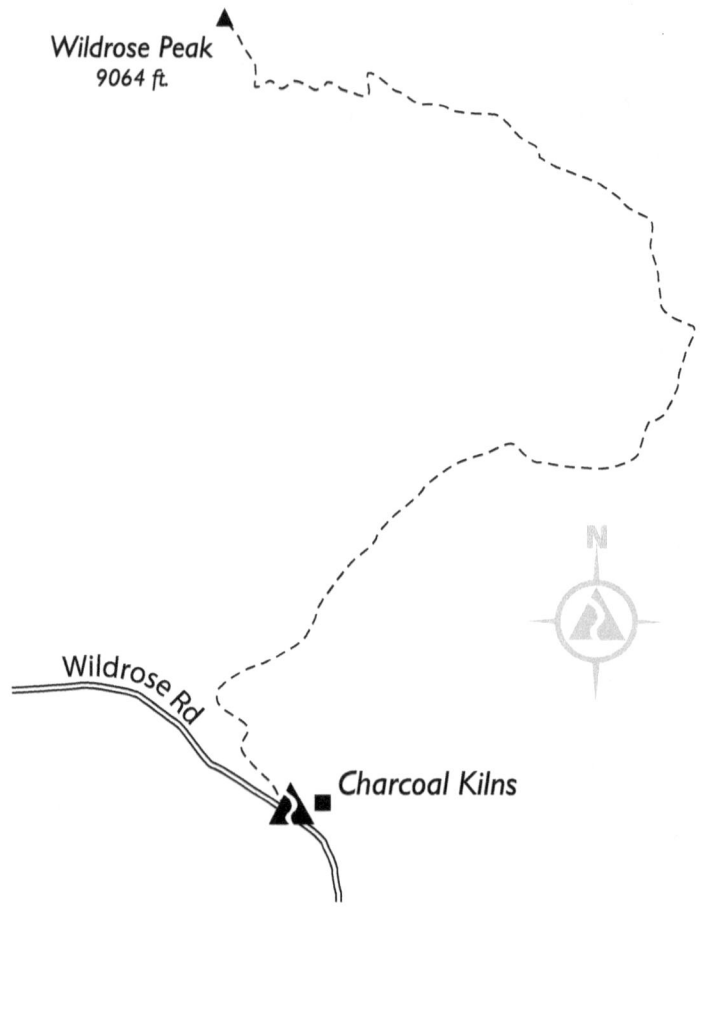

Wildrose Peak

Wildrose Peak Trail

8.4 miles round trip with 2,300-foot elevation gain

Death Valley and Panamint Valley views are awesome from the summit of Wildrose Peak. The 9,064-foot peak in the middle of the Panamint Mountains beckons the hiker with a well-maintained trail and glorious views coming and going.

The Panamints are known as the wettest mountain range in Death Valley—a small claim to fame to be sure in the midst of one of America's most arid lands; nevertheless, there's enough precipitation in the form of rain and snow to nurture stands of pinyon pine and juniper, and water the "wildrose," the spring-blooming cliff-rose that brightens the mountain.

In summer, when temperatures are unbearable on the floor of Death Valley, Wildrose Peak remains a pleasant place to hike. The peak and upper parts of the trail are snowbound in winter; however Wildrose is walkable a bit earlier in spring than neighboring

Telescope Peak (11,049 feet), which typically remains mantled in snow well into May. It's often very windy atop Wildrose Peak so dress accordingly.

The trailhead alone is worth the trip. Here you'll find ten charcoal kilns, built in the 1870s to make charcoal from the trees growing in Wildrose Canyon. Charcoal was carried from the giant beehive-shaped stone kilns by mules to the Modock Mine, located in the Argus Range, 25 miles away.

DIRECTIONS: From Highway 190 and Panamint Valley Road, some 50 miles from Highway 395, turn right at the signed paved road for Wildrose and proceed 9.5 miles northwest to a junction with Mahogany Flat Road. Turn right, soon passing Wildrose Campground, and travel 7 miles (the last 2.5 miles on dirt road) to a wide turnout for the charcoal kilns and parking for Wildrose Peak-bound hikers.

If you're journeying from the "main" part of Death Valley, travel 9 miles from Stovepipe Wells south on Highway 190 to Wildrose Road. Turn left and drive south 21 miles to Mahogany Flat Road.

THE HIKE: Join the signed trail northwest of the charcoal kilns and begin your ascent above Wildrose Canyon. As you pass in and out of a pinyon and juniper woodland, enjoy the great views of High Sierra peaks, including mighty Mt. Whitney. The path descends briefly into a wooded canyon, then climbs northeast.

Wildrose Peak

About two miles out the path reaches a saddle at the crest of the Panamints. Following the crest, the trail serves up great vistas of Death Valley shimmering in the heat 8,000 feet below, as well as over-the-shoulder views of Telescope Peak. The trail leads to a second saddle at the 3-mile mark and more great panoramas.

Vigorous switchbacks lead past wind-bent pinyon pine to a false summit on Wildrose's south peak then the small, flat, and true summit on its north peak. The fantastic view takes in most of 90-mile long Death Valley with the Amargosa Range beyond and Furnace Creek appearing as a green island on the vast salt flats. To the west are the saw-tooth summits of the Sierra Nevada.

Wildrose Peak, in the middle of the Panamint Range, offers grand views of Death Valley and the High Sierra.

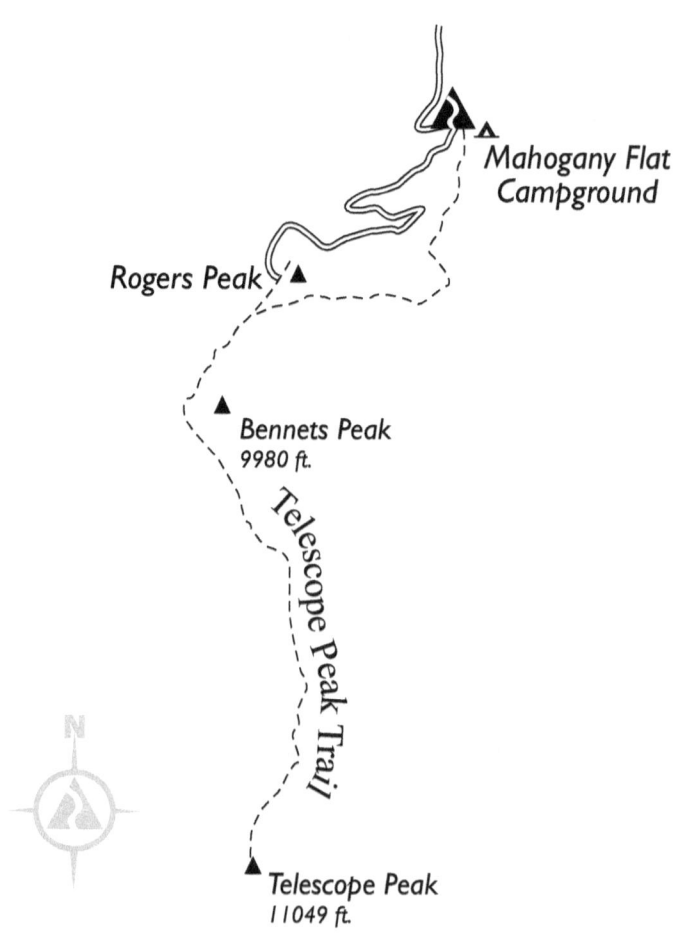

Telescope Peak
Telescope Peak Trail

To Telescope Peak is 14 miles round trip with 3,000-foot gain

Most park visitors are content to stop their cars at Badwater, 282 feet below sea level and look up at Telescope Peak, the greatest vertical rise in the lower 48 states. For the true hiker, however, the challenge of climbing 11,049-foot Telescope Peak and looking down at Death Valley will prove irresistible.

Views from Telescope Peak Trail include Badwater, low point of the continental U.S. and Mt. Whitney, the continental high point. The 360-degree panorama inspired one W.T. Henderson, first to ascend the great mountain in 1860, to declare: "You can see so far, it's just like looking through a telescope."

The trail starts where most trails end—a mile and a half in the sky—and climbs a sagebrush- and pinyon pine-dotted hogback ridge to the pinnacle that is Telescope Peak.

Best time to hike Telescope Peak is from mid-May to November. During the colder months, much of the trail is covered in snow.

DIRECTIONS: From Highway 190 and Panamint Valley Road, some 50 miles from Highway 395, turn right on Wildrose Canyon Road and follow it 9 miles to road's end at Mahogany Flat Campground. The signed trail begins at the south end of the campground.

THE HIKE: The path climbs over pinyon pine-forested slopes and soon offers dramatic views of Death Valley and the Furnace Creek area. Sign in at the trail register located about a quarter-mile from the trailhead. After 2 miles, the trail gains the spine of a ridge and soon a second valley, Panamint, comes into view.

After about 2.7 miles of moderate climbing from the trailhead, reach a saddle between Rogers Peak and Bennett Peak. Typically, this part of the trail is snow-covered in winter, and sometimes into the first weeks of May. (You can strike cross-country to reach the antennae-crowned summit of Rogers Peak, which stands about 400-feet higher than the trail.)

Continue on the main trail to a second saddle south of 9,980-foot Bennett Peak, about 4.3 miles from the trailhead at an elevation of 9,500 feet.

Telescope Peak Trail's final third is steep and remarkable. The path zigzags up the peak's steep east side, ascending through a stunted forest of limber and bristlecone pine. About 6 miles out, at 10,500 feet, pass wonderfully statuesque bristlecones, ancients estimated to be about 3,000 years old.

About a quarter-mile short of the peak, reach the 11,000-foot mark and trek the windswept ridge over two bumps to reach a third, the summit promontory.

From atop the peak, marvel at the magnificent vistas from the below-sea level salt pans, including Badwater, to the high snowy summits of the Sierra Nevada. The far-reaching views also include the White Mountains to the north and the Inyo Mountains. Off in those two patches of purple haze are Las Vegas far to the east and the San Gabriel Mountains above Los Angeles to the southwest.

Get high above Death Valley on Telescope Peak, the greatest vertical rise in the contiguous United States.

Ronald Reagan was a host of the
long-running TV series "Death Valley Days"
that aired from 1952 to 1970.

EVERY TRAIL TELLS A STORY.

Death Valley Stories

HIKE ON.

White Heart of the Mojave
By Edna Brush Perkins

Author Edna Brush Perkins in 1922 when her "White Heart of the Mojave" was published.

With the hope of leaving political struggles and civilization far behind, ardent suffragette and plucky adventurer Edna Brush Perkins set out in 1920 with her friend Charlotte to journey into the Mojave, Her exploration of Death Valley is particularly evocative, and she emerged from the trip profoundly changed.

There was supposed to be a road, but neither Charlotte nor I could discern it. We bumped along over ground so cut by shallow water-channels that after about seven miles we dared not proceed, for a wrecked car in that shining desolation would stay forever where it smashed. We tried to walk to the top of the gravel-ridge that seemed to shut off the main valley. It looked near and innocent enough, but when we tried to reach it over the dazzling ground under the blazing sun we found, to our surprise, that we could not. The temperature was about 95 degrees, and the air very dry. The heat alone would have been quite bearable had it not been augmented by the white glare.

Suddenly we realized that the little ridge was inaccessible; all the little yellow hills and ridges, and the rocky crests that shone like burnished metal, were likewise inaccessible. The realization brought a terrifying sense of helplessness. Here was a country you could not travel over: though your goal were in sight you might never reach it. The strength and resourcefulness you relied on for emergencies were of no avail; an empty canteen, a lost burro, a smashed car, and your history might be finished. We began to understand why this place, so gay with color, so flooded with light, so clean, so bright, was called Death Valley.

Before us was the opening in the mountains where the terrible valley itself lay. It was magnificent in the biggest sense of that big, ill-used word. On the east side rose the precipitous Panamints with a thin line of snow on their summits; opposite them the dark buttresses of the Funeral Mountains faded back into dimness. Between the ranges hung a blue haze of the quality of the sky, like the haze that had obscured the hot Imperial Valley.

The mountains were majestic, immovable, their summits dwelt in the living silence. The haze had the magicalness of mirage. We longed to go on while the sun went down and the silence turned blue, for now we were certain that under the haze, between those imposing walls, lay the climax to which Mojave had been leading us, her White Heart. She could never be more desolate, or stiller or grander. It was the logical journey's end, and what had been at first merely a casual choice of destination became a fixed goal to be reached through any hazards.

"If you go there," the old prospector had said, "you will see something you won't see anywhere else on earth."

Death Valley WPA Guide

In the 1930s, auto tours were popular with visitors eager to see the sights in the new Death Valley National Monument.

Death Valley: A Guide was written in 1938 as part of the American Guide Series produced by the Federal Writers' Project. Primary writer Cora Vernon Lee insisted on working in the heat of summer for the most authentic experience possible.

Ever since the first immigrants saw Death Valley, fantastic tales have been told of its blasting temperatures and stupendous riches, but exaggeration is inevitable in describing this narrow valley of strange, exciting beauty, cradled between towering varicolored mountains, Indians, immigrants, prospectors, miners—all have paused here and left traces; but the Valley, formed by mighty earth movements and sculptured by wind and water, retains a sublime impersonality that has changed little in a million years.

Death Valley, part of the Great American Desert, is largely in southeastern California. In 1933 Death Valley National Monument was established to preserve the area. The Monument contains 2981 square miles, 500 of which are below sea level. Prior to 1933, Death Valley was largely cared for by the Pacific Coast Borax Company which still conducts the hotels, camps, service stations, and other facilities at Death Valley Junction and Furnace Creek Inn.

The 140-mile curved trough of the Valley lies between steep mountain walls of naked rock, barbaric in coloring. Because it is only six to fifteen miles wide, the vivid rock mountains always rim the horizon. In winter they rear up from the narrow floor in somber splendor; in summer they shimmer in the heat haze that rises from the white pit at their feet. At times their varied hues have the transparent brilliance of incandescent metal—reds, blues, greens, brown, lilac, purples—and tans, pinks, and grays are splashed and streaked along their sides. This flamboyant coloring does not disturb the great peace and serenity that are the special qualities of Death Valley. The desert quiet is scarcely broken by small, whispering winds and by occasional bird notes. The sky is usually a clear, light blue, but when it is clouded the sunsets are unbelievably gorgeous. At night stars, large in the black velvet sky, roll slowly toward the west.

Death Valley is divided into two shallow basins by a range of low hills. In the southern basin are the great shimmering Salt Beds; here is the lowest spot in North America, Badwater, 279.6 feet below sea level—only eighty miles away from the highest point in any of the 48 States, Mount Whitney, which rises 14,495 feet above the sea. Both Mount Whitney and Badwater are seen from Dante's View in the Black Mountains.

In a world of constant change, where cities rise swiftly in wild places, where green forests turn overnight to ash heaps or black scars, where fertile prairies become shifting dust, Death Valley changes little from decade to decade; its desert plants seem no fewer, no more, and little vagrant winds continue to carry the same faint, dry odor of earth and rock, and to sing the same soft, tuneless songs. Everything in the Valley seems constant but color; it varies with the changing light, ranging through an infinite variety of tones, from the bleached, exhausted ones seen under the blazing summer sun to the rich hues that glow in splendor under the low gray sky of a winter day.

Death Valley: A Misnomer of Grand Proportions

Death Valley was a sentimental favorite of Horace Albright, a founding father of the National Park Service.

"Death Valley: A Misnomer of Grand Proportions" by John McKinney
(*California Scenic Magazine*, October 1987)

"Death Valley National Park was in many ways a tough sell," admitted Horace Albright, a founding father of the National Park Service. After all, he explained, in the early 1930s, the general public—and most members of Congress regarded Death Valley as a trackless wasteland. And President Hoover came from a mining background, and often tilted more toward industry than scenery.

A half-century after Death Valley became national parkland, Horace Albright told me a story; the recollection made him smile. "I think," he said, with a twinkle in his eye, "the public would be surprised to find out what goes on in a place like Death Valley before them. Park Service puts up its welcome signs."

Early in 1933, National Park Service director Albright was at work in his Washington office on the presidential proclamation for Death Valley National Monument. In walked Chicago millionaire Albert Johnson, backer of Death Valley Scotty, a colorful local character, and the moneyman behind Scotty's Castle. Johnson had a serious problem: a government survey had revealed that he didn't own the land where his castle stood. The land he had bought was actually a mile away, and the castle land belonged to the government, which intended to create a national park. Would Albright mind excluding his land and castle from the new national park?

Johnson described his castle in glowing terms, how it seemed to rise like a mirage from the desolation of Grapevine Canyon. He described the Spanish tile roofs, fountains, baronial dining hall, huge chandeliers, hand-tooled leather curtains, the oil paintings and tapestries.

Albright decided to have a little fun. "The way you described it," he told Johnson, "that castle would be wonderful for park headquarters.

Johnson was crestfallen, even more so when Albright, with a mischievous grin, opined that one of those fancy rooms would make a splendid western field office for him. Johnson was inconsolable by the time Albright confessed that he was only joking and promised to exclude the castle ground from the park.

Park? What was 1932 Congress thinking when it passed legislation placing Death Valley under National Park Service stewardship? The word "park" bespeaks of governance (beauty and bureaucracy are always the strangest of bedfellows), and a strange concept in a strange land. This territory is an ungovernable as its flaming sunsets.

Recently my thoughts have turned to the story of Death Valley as a park, and to Horace Albright, one of the greats of the American conservation movement, who helped bring Death Valley and a far-flung collection of other scenic gems under the protection of the National Park Service.

In 1913, Albright interrupted his study of mining law at the University of California to take a job in Washington as confidential clerk to the Secretary of the Interior. He soon teamed with wealthy borax industry executive Stephen Mather to establish the National Park Service, serving as superintendent of Yellowstone National Park and as Mather's field representative. For nearly two decades, Albright explored and evaluated dozens of potential parks and historical sites. The Park Service lost a founding father, and the American landscape a great friend when Horace Albright died this year at the age of 97.

One of his favorite parks was Death Valley. Like a proud father with many children, he'd never name a favorite, but Death Valley always occupied a special place in his heart. His upbringing in the nearby town of Bishop, his interest in mining, and his major role in the park's creation, all contributed to his love of the valley. When I asked him about the attraction of Death Valley, he adjusted his hat, pulled on his string tie, and said suddenly: "The rocks. You can see almost the whole history of the earth in those rocks."

Director Albright insisted only the best be hired for the new National Park Service, like Death Valley Ranger John Bergen, shown here at Badwater in 1935.

Death Valley in '49

During the 1849 California Gold Rush, William Lewis Manly rescued several pioneer families from Death Valley. Manly's autobiographical *Death Valley in 49* tells of the sufferings of the lost pioneers who gave "Death Valley" its name.

Three prominent features in Death Valley bear his name: Manly Beacon (near Zabriskie Point), Manly Peak and Lake Manly. The story of Manley's heroic rescues was told in the first episode of the TV series, "Death Valley Days."

William Lewis Manly (1820-1903) rescued pioneers lost in Death Valley.

Most seemed to think that to stay was to die, and it would be better to die trying to escape than to set idly down to perish.

There was no end to the questions about the road we had to answer, for this was uppermost on their minds, and we tried to tell them and show them how we must get along on our return. We told them of the great snow mountains we had seen all to the north of our road, and how deep the snow appeared to be, and how far west it extended. We told them of the black and desolate ranges and buttes to the south, and of the great dry plains in the same direction.

We told them of the Jayhawkers trail; of Fish's dead body; of the salt lake and slippery alkali water to which we walked, only to turn away in disappointment; of the discouraged ones who gave us their names to send back to friends.

Our sad adventures and loss of the horses in returning was sorrowfully told and we spoke of the provisions we had been able to bring on the little mule which had clambered over the rocks like a cat; that we had a little flour and beans, and some good dried meat with fat on it which we hoped would help to eke out the poorer fare and get them through at last.

They were so full of compliments that we really began to think we had been brought into the world on purpose to assist someone, and the one who could forecast all things had directed us, and all our ways, so that we should save those people and bring them to a better part of God's footstool, where plenty might be enjoyed, and the sorrows of the desert forgotten.

Land of Little Rain

Early nature writer and champion of indigenous people, the prolific Mary Hunter Austin is best known for her classic *The Land of Little Rain* (1903), an account of the fauna, flora, and people of the desert, as well as its mystical attraction.

Here you find the hot sink of Death Valley, or high rolling districts where the air has always a tang of frost. Here are the long heavy winds and breathless calms on the tilted mesas where dust devils dance, whirling up into a wide, pale sky. Here you have no rain when all the earth cries for it, or quick downpours called cloudbursts for violence. A land of lost rivers, with little in it to love; yet a land that once visited must be come back to inevitably. If it were not so there would be little told of it.

The desert floras shame us with their cheerful adaptations to the seasonal limitations. Their whole duty is to flower and fruit, and they do it hardly, or with tropical luxuriance, as the rain admits. It is recorded in the report of the Death Valley expedition that after a year of abundant rains, on the Colorado desert was found a specimen of Amaranthus ten feet high. A year later the same species in the same place matured in the drought at four inches. Extreme aridity and extreme altitude have the same dwarfing effect, so that we find in the high Sierras and in Death Valley related species in miniature that reach a comely growth in mean temperatures. Very fertile are the desert plants in expedients to prevent evaporation, turning their foliage edgewise toward the sun, growing silky hairs, exuding viscid gum. The wind, which has a long sweep, harries and helps them. It rolls up dunes about the stocky stems, encompassing and protective, and above the dunes, which may be, as with the mesquite, three times as high as a man, the blossoming twigs flourish and bear fruit.

If you have any doubt about it, know that the desert begins with the creosote. This immortal shrub spreads down into Death Valley and up to the lower timberline, odorous and medicinal as you might guess from the name, wand like, with shining fretted foliage. Its vivid green is grateful to the eye in a wilderness of gray and greenish white shrubs. In the spring it exudes a resinous gum which the Indians of those parts know how to use with pulverized rock for cementing arrow points to shafts. Trust Indians not to miss any virtues of the plant world!

There are many areas in the desert where drinkable water lies within a few feet of the surface, indicated by the mesquite and the bunch grass. It is this nearness of unimagined help that makes the tragedy of desert deaths. It is related that the final breakdown of that hapless party that gave Death Valley its forbidding name occurred in a locality where shallow wells would have saved them. But how were they to know that? Properly equipped it is possible to go safely across that ghastly sink, yet every year it takes its toll of death, and yet men find there sun-dried mummies, of whom no trace or recollection is preserved. To underestimate one's thirst, to pass a given landmark to the right or left, to find a dry spring where one looked for running water—there is no help for any of these things.

Death Valley NP
LAVA BEDS NM
YOSEMITE NATIONAL PARK
César Chávez NM
Joshua Tree National Park
Pinnacles NP
EUGENE O'NEIL NHS
MUIR WOODS NM
Whiskeytown-Shasta Trinity NRA
Golden Gate National Recreation Area
REDWOOD NP
CHANNEL ISLANDS NATIONAL PARK
DEVILS POSTPILE NM
LASSEN VOLCANIC NATIONAL PARK
Cabrillo NM
MOJAVE NPRES
John Muir NHS
Rosie the Riveter NHS
Santa Monica Mountains NRA
POINT REYES NS
SEQUOIA-KINGS CANYON NATIONAL PARKS

California's National Parks

Other states have national parks with tall trees, high peaks, deep canyons, long seashores and vast deserts, but only California can claim all these grand landscapes within its boundaries.

California boasts nine national parks, the most in the nation. In addition, the state's national parklands include national recreation areas, national monuments, national historic parks, a national seashore and a national preserve.

The state features one of America's oldest national parks—Yosemite set aside in 1890—and one of its newest—César E. Chávez National Monument established in 2012.

Mere acreage does not a national park make, but California's national parks include the largest park in the contiguous U.S.—3.3-million acre Death Valley National Park. Yosemite (748,542 acres) and Joshua Tree (790,636 acres) are also huge by any park standards. Even such smaller parklands as Redwoods National Park and Pt. Reyes National Seashore are by no means small.

California and The National Park Idea

Not long after John Muir walked through Mariposa Grove and into the Yosemite Valley, California's natural treasures attracted attention worldwide and conservationists rallied to preserve them as parks. As the great naturalist put it in 1898: "Thousands of nerve-shaken, overcivilized people are beginning to find out that going to the mountains is going home; that wilderness is a necessity; and that mountain parks and reservations are useful not only as fountains of timber and irrigating rivers, but as fountains of life."

The National Park Service, founded in 1916, was initially guided by borax tycoon-turned-park-champion Stephen T. Mather and his young assistant, California attorney Horace Albright. The park service's mission was the preservation of "the scenery and the natural and historic objects and the wild life" and the provision "for the enjoyment of the same in such manner and by such means as will leave them unimpaired for the enjoyment of future generations."

The invention of the automobile revolutionized national park visitation, particularly in car-conscious California. John Muir called them "blunt-nosed mechanical beetles," yet as one California senator pointed out, "If Jesus Christ had an automobile he wouldn't have ridden a jackass into Jerusalem."

With cars came trailers, and with trailer camps came concessionaires. National parks filled with mobile cities of canvas and aluminum, and by visitors anxious to see California's natural wonders. During the 1920s and 30s, the park service constructed signs identifying scenic features and rangers assumed the role of interpreting nature for visitors.

By 1930 California had four national parks: Yosemite, Lassen, Sequoia and General Grant (Kings Canyon.) In the 1930s, two big desert areas—Joshua Tree and Death Valley—became national monuments.

With the 1960s came hotly contested, and eventually successful campaigns to create Redwood National

Steven Mather (R) and his assistant Horace Albright guided the National Park Service in its early days.

Park and Point Reyes National Seashore. During the 1970s the National Park Service established parks near the state's big cities—Golden Gate National Recreation Area on the San Francisco waterfront and Marin headlands and Santa Monica Mountains National Recreation Area, a Mediterranean ecosystem near Los Angeles. Also during that decade, Mineral King Valley was saved from a mega-ski resort development and added to Sequoia National Park. Channel Islands National Park, an archipelago offshore from Santa Barbara, was established in 1980.

During the 1980s and 1990s, major conservation battles raged in the desert. After more than two decades of wrangling, Joshua Tree and Death Valley national monuments were greatly expanded and given national park status, and the 1.6-million acre Mojave National Preserve was established under provisions of the 1994 California Desert Conservation Act.

Today, the National Park Service must address challenging questions: How best to regulate concessionaires? Should motor vehicles be banned from Yosemite Valley? How can aging park facilities cope with many years of deferred maintenance?

And the biggest issue of all: How will our parks (indeed our planet!) cope with the rapidly increasing effects of climate change?

The consequences of climate change to California's national parks is ever more apparent. In recent years, after prolonged droughts, devastating wildfires burned the Yosemite backcountry, parts of Sequoia National Park and more than half the Santa Monica Mountains National Recreation Area. Scientists have discovered that trees in Sequoia and Kings Canyon national parks endure the worst ozone levels of all national parks, in part because of their proximity to farm-belt air in the San Joaquin Valley.

California's national parklands struggle with an ever-increasing numbers of visitors. The California Office of Tourism charts visitation to national parks along with airports, hotel occupancy and other attractions such as Disneyland and Universal Studios. Yosemite is California's most-visited park with 4.5 to 5 million visitors a year, and many other parks count millions of visitors or "visitor days," per year.

What may be the saving grace of national parks is the deep-seated, multi-generational pride Americans have for their national parklands. We not only love national parks, we love the very idea of national parks. Even in an era of public mistrust toward government, national parks remain one of the most beloved institutions of American life.

National Parks have often been celebrated as America's best idea. As writer Wallace Stegner put it: "National parks are the best idea we ever had. Absolutely American, absolutely democratic, they reflect us at our best rather than our worst."

The Trails

The state of the state's national park trail system is excellent. Trailhead parking, interpretive panels and displays, as well as signage, is generally tops in the field. Backcountry junctions are usually signed and trail conditions, with a few exceptions of course, range from good to excellent.

Trail systems evolved on a park-by-park basis and it's difficult to speak in generalities about their respective origins. A good deal of Yosemite's trail system was in place before the early horseless carriages chugged into the park.

Several national parks were aided greatly by the Depression-era Civilian Conservation Corps of the 1930s. Sequoia and Pinnacles national parks, for example, have hand-built trails by the CCC that are true gems, highlighted by stonework and bridges that would no doubt be prohibitively expensive to construct today.

Scout troops, the hard-working young men and women of the California Conservation Corps and many volunteer groups are among the organizations that help park staff build and maintain trails.

The trail system in California's national parklands shares many characteristics in common with pathways overseen by other governmental bodies, and have unique qualities as well. One major difference between national parks and, for example, California's state parks, is the amount of land preserved as wilderness. A majority of Yosemite, Sequoia, Death Valley, Joshua Tree and several more parks are official federally designated wilderness. Wilderness comprises some 94 percent of Yosemite National Park, 93 percent of Death Valley National Park, and more than 80 percent of Joshua Tree National Park.

On national park maps you'll find wilderness areas delineated as simply "Wilderness." Unlike the Forest Service, the Bureau of Land Management or other wilderness stewards, the National Park Service does not name its wilderness areas.

Author John McKinney admires the sign for Yosemite's Four Mile Trail.

"Wilderness" is more than a name for a wild area. By law, a wilderness is restricted to non-motorized entry—that is to say, equestrian and foot travel. Happily, hikers do not have to share the trails with snowmobiles or mountain bikes in national park wilderness.

Because national park trails attract visitors from all over the globe, the park service makes use of international symbols on its signage, and the metric system as well. Don't be surprised if you spot trail signs with distance expressed in kilometers as well as miles and elevation noted in meters as well as feet.

The hikers you meet on a national park trail may be different from the company you keep on trails near home. California's national parks attract increasing numbers of ethnically and culturally diverse hikers of all ages, shapes and sizes, from across the nation and around the world. Once I counted ten languages on a popular trail in Yosemite! The hiking experience is much enriched by sharing the trail with hikers from literally all walks of life.

California's National Parklands

Alcatraz Island
Cabrillo National Monument
Castle Mountains National Monument
César E. Chávez National Monument
Channel Islands National Park
Death Valley National Park
Devils Postpile National Monument
Eugene O'Neill National Historic Site
Fort Point National Historic Site
Golden Gate National Recreation Area
John Muir National Historic Site
Joshua Tree National Park
Lassen Volcanic National Park
Lava Beds National Monument
Manzanar National Historic Site
Mojave National Preserve
Muir Woods National Monument
Pinnacles National Park
Point Reyes National Seashore
Port Chicago Naval Magazine National Memorial
Presidio of San Francisco
Redwood National and State Parks
Rosie the Riveter WWII Home Front National
    Historic Park
San Francisco Maritime National Historic Park
Santa Monica Mountains National Recreation Area
Sequoia and Kings Canyon National Parks
Tule Lake National Monument
Whiskeytown National Recreation Area
Yosemite National Park

The Hiker's Index

Celebrating the Scenic, Sublime and Sensational Points of Interest in California's National Parks

State with the most National Parks

California, with 9

Largest National Park in Contiguous U.S.

Death Valley with 3.3 million acres

Third Largest National Park in Contiguous U.S.

Mojave National Preserve

Foggiest Place on the West Coast

Point Reyes Lighthouse, Point Reyes National Seashore

World's Tallest Tree

A 379.7-foot high coast redwood named Hyperion in Redwood National Park

World's Largest Tree

General Sherman Tree, 275 feet tall, with a base circumference of 102 feet, growing in the Giant Forest Area of Sequoia National Park

World's Largest-In-Diameter Tree

General Grant Tree, dubbed "the nation's Christmas tree," more than 40 feet in diameter at its base, growing in Kings Canyon National Park.

Largest Elephant Seal Population on Earth

San Miguel Island, Channel Islands National Park

Highest Point in Contiguous U.S.

Mt. Whitney (14,508 feet in elevation) on the far eastern boundary of Sequoia National Park

Lowest Point in Western Hemisphere

Badwater (282 feet below sea level) in Death Valley National Park

California's Largest Island

Santa Cruz Island, Channel Islands National Park

Only Major Metropolis Bisected by a Mountain Range

Los Angeles, by the Santa Monica Mountains (National Recreation Area)

Highest Waterfall in North America

Yosemite Falls, at 2,425 feet, in Yosemite National Park

JOHN MCKINNEY

John McKinney is an award-winning writer, public speaker, and author of 30 hiking-themed books: inspiring narratives, top-selling guides, books for children.

John is particularly passionate about sharing the stories of California trails. He is the only one to have visited—and written about—all 280 California State Parks. John tells the story of his epic hike along the entire California coast in the critically acclaimed *Hiking on the Edge: Dreams, Schemes, and 1600 Miles on the California Coastal Trail.*

For 18 years John, aka The Trailmaster, wrote a weekly hiking column for the Los Angeles Times, and has hiked and enthusiastically told the story of more than 10 thousand miles of trail across California and around the world. His "Every Trail Tells a Story" series of guides highlight the very best hikes in California.

The intrepid Eagle Scout has written more than a thousand stories and opinion pieces about hiking, parklands, and our relationship with nature.

A passionate advocate for hiking and our need to reconnect with nature, John is a frequent public speaker, and shares his tales on radio, on video, and online.

JOHN MCKINNEY:
"EVERY TRAIL TELLS A STORY."

Hike On.

TheTrailmaster.com

www.ingramcontent.com/pod-product-compliance
Lightning Source LLC
Chambersburg PA
CBHW032041290426
44110CB00012B/906